Question: Wh[...]
Answer: Jon[...]

Q: What year is [...]
A: 1844

Q: How old are you?
A: Ten.

What makes the above exchange so remarkable is that it took place *not* in 1844 but over 120 years later, and that the boy speaking is actually named George Field, age 15, not 10.

Under deep hypnosis George Field regressed to a previous life as a farm boy in North Carolina. Incredibly, when in this trance, he was able to name a local river, a neighbor, the traveling minister, a local store, and dozens of other traceable items. A follow-up trip to the town George Field said he had lived in during another, an earlier, lifetime backed up his statements to a startling degree.

Was this mere coincidence? The chances are staggeringly against it. Could it be post-hypnotic suggestion? Hardly. Over and over again—under carefully controlled conditions—hypnotist Loring Williams (who had worked with George Field as well as with the numerous other persons cited in this book) proved that no subject was "helped" in any way.

This book contains the transcripts that recorded exactly what happened during the hypnotic sessions which tested the theory of reincarnation—so you may judge for yourself!

OTHER LIVES

Brad Steiger
and
Loring G. Williams

AWARD BOOKS
NEW YORK

TANDEM BOOKS
LONDON

FIRST AWARD PRINTING 1969

AWARD BOOKS are published by
Universal Publishing and Distributing Corporation
235 East Forty-fifth Street, New York, N.Y. 10017

TANDEM BOOKS are published by
Universal-Tandem Publishing Company Limited
14 Gloucester Road, London SW7, England

Manufactured in the United States of America

CONTENTS

AUTHOR'S FOREWORD

I first became familiar with Loring G. Williams and his experimental work when I read his article "Reincarnation of a Civil War Victim" in the December, 1966, issue of *Fate* magazine. In a case recounted in that article, Williams used hypnotic techniques to regress a New Hampshire high school boy further than memory of the birth experience and back to a life which he claimed to have led as a farmer in Jefferson, North Carolina, some time between 1840 to 1863. When I finished reading the article I was surprised and excited. Loring G. Williams had offered the reader more than a fascinating story; he had presented some thoroughly documented proof of his subject's former incarnation.

I had studied various "scientific" reports which debunked hypnotist Morey Bernstein's famed search for Bridey Murphy; but I was also cognizant of Professor C. J. Ducasse's brilliant analysis which demonstrated that the regressed subject, Mrs. Virginia Tighe, revealed facts about Ireland which were at first unfamiliar even to the experts and that if Bridey Murphy were not an actual personality then Mrs. Tighe gained this information through paranormal means. I was also aware of the study of Dr. E. S. Zolik which demonstrated the facility with which hypnotized subjects can be instructed to "remember" fictitious previous lives. Then, too, I personally have conducted a long study of the guide, or "control," of the spirit medium; and I had wondered if such a product of the unconscious or the spirit world might not

7

explain many cases of alleged reincarnation. In brief, I was confused about the whole matter of reincarnation and about the validity of any hypnotically regressed subject who produced an account of a former life.

But in Loring G. Williams, I had encountered a New England high school teacher who enjoyed a reputation as a hypnotist of remarkable ability, who had not only regressed a young man to what appeared to be a former life, but who had taken the subject to the actual scene of the alleged incarnation in his efforts to substantiate the story. "Jonathan Powell" had presented Williams with clear details of the events of his life, and Williams had been able to check out many of them before undertaking the psychic safari to Jefferson, N. C. On the actual ground that Jonathan claimed to have walked a hundred years earlier, Williams went through the county records, talked with local historians, and was able to accumulate a great deal of confirming evidence. Here was no imaginative fantasy spun by some creative facet of a hypnotized subject's unconscious; here were facts to prove the subject's former life.

I contacted "Bill" Williams and found him most willing to cooperate with me on a book that would cover several aspects of the mystery of reincarnation and present a wide range of theories, research and philosophical viewpoints. Bill sent me additional materials which he had accumulated since the Jonathan case, and I included a chapter on Williams' work in my previous book *The Enigma of Reincarnation*.

In the introduction to that earlier book I made clear my position regarding the question of rebirth. I stated that I did believe man and his mind were something other than physical things, but that my entire intellectual, emotional and religious bias had always inclined me against reincarnation. I had been compelled to write the book, I explained, because of an irritating number of cases which held up under the most exacting analyses and because of the many great thinkers who, through the ages, have professed their belief in the ethics of Karma and the reality of reincarnation.

After that book was released, I received a call from Bill

Williams, who told me that I had to hear the tape recordings he had made of some new cases in progress. "Typed transcripts are just not enough," Williams told me. "You have to hear these people reliving their past lives, suffering through the death experience, being reinstated on earth through the birth experience. Once you hear the genuine emotion in those voices, you'll be convinced that these subjects are reliving former lives, and not simply acting out fantasies."

I listened to the new tapes. If I was not immediately convinced of their validity, I was enormously impressed with the dramatic intensity of the phenomenon. I was certain that Bill had not established a New Hampshire repertory company of superb amateur actors, but I found it difficult to accept the hypnotist's assessment that his subjects were indeed reliving past lives. I did, however, know one thing with absolute certainty: I had to do a book with Bill Williams on cases of hypnotic regression which seemed suggestive of reincarnation.

I was no longer teaching in college, but had embarked on a full-time exploration of the strange and unknown. Bill Williams was committed by his teacher's contract to stay put in New Hampshire, but we would have the summer to spend in research. In the meantime, we would correspond and I would learn all that I could about hypnosis and diligently gather more material on the fascinating subject of reincarnation.

I learned from Bill's letters, as I later learned from firsthand observation, that the subject who is regressed to an ostensible former life actually relives that life in a manner that surpasses simple remembering. He feels the same pain; he sees familiar objects; he uses colloquial expressions, although not always with an expected accent. He either does not see or does not recognize anything modern. Instead he sees the period to which he has been regressed. If the hypnotist calls his attention to something modern, the subject seems dismayed with it for he is actually living in another era.

At first one might suppose that such an emotionally draining process would cause the subject distress after he had been brought out of the hypnotic trance. But there is no such effect, because there is no memory of what has taken place. If the subject should audit a tape recording of his session, he may find it interesting or entertaining, but he will not feel that it is really he.

As with any potent instrument, one must exercise caution and common sense when working with hypnosis. There is always the possibility that the regressed subject may relive a traumatic experience. Here the hypnotist must know his technique well enough to recognize—by facial expressions and other signs—such psychically supercharged areas and to carry the subject quickly around such experiences.

Loring G. Williams considers hypnosis to be the "key that unlocks the door" to great progress in the field of psychical research. "Contrary to widespread belief," Williams explained, "hypnosis is not a sleep. It is a trance state in which the words of the hypnotist reach beyond the subject's conscious to his unconscious. The hypnotist, then, communicates directly with the unconscious mind."

Survival after death and the nature of death itself are subjects which have been considered by mankind's greatest minds. In the midst of his sufferings, Job asked: "If a man die, shall he live again?"

The search for the Great Answer continues in many ways and is led by many people. Among these is soft-spoken, Yankee-practical Bill Williams, whose method is to ask his subjects, at the count of three, to journey back through time and space.

—*Brad Steiger*

CHAPTER I

THE REINCARNATION OF JONATHAN POWELL

The young man's expression of angry defiance was suddenly clouded by fear. "Oh!" he gasped, doubling over in pain. "They shot me! Those damn Yankee soldiers shot me!"

Tears streamed down his face. "I wouldn't take ... their money. I wouldn't take their damn money for my potatoes My stomach ... they shot me in the stomach."

Within a few moments a look of peace had crossed his face, and the painful gasping stopped. Jonathan Powell was dead.

"Now what do you feel?" asked the hypnotist.

"Nothing," Jonathan answered in a puzzled tone. "I can't feel anything. I can't see a darn thing."

The hypnotist spoke again, soothingly, to calm the panic that showed in Jonathan's speech. "There's nothing to fear. On the count of three you will come back to the present time. One ... two ... three!"

The small North Carolina marketplace was instantly transformed into the comfortable New Hampshire living room of Loring G. Williams. The year was no longer 1863, but 1965. The mortally wounded Jonathan Powell had reawakened as a smiling and somewhat perplexed George Field.

"Did I say anything?" the teenager asked. "Did I say anything at all?"

Williams clicked off the tape recorder. "Yes," he answered. "You certainly did."

The New Hampshire schoolteacher has long been interested in hypnosis, particularly in age regression. It has been well established that some people can be hypnotically regressed to their early childhood to relive past experiences. In this state, good hypnotic subjects are able to accurately describe remembered people, places, and events as if they were actual. It has been Williams' experience that in practically all cases in which the subject can be regressed to childhood, he also can be regressed beyond childhood to the birth experience. In many instances these same people can be regressed beyond the birth experience to recall and describe what appear to be other lives.

In his home early in 1965, Williams began holding weekly sessions during which volunteers were hypnotized and regressed. It was Williams' hope to find a subject whose story could be checked and substantiated. A pragmatic Yankee schoolteacher, Williams was well aware that, however fascinating it might be to hear and to record stories of alleged former lives, such material was of little value unless the stories could be established to be true. And now he had discovered "Jonathan Powell" in the person of fifteen-year-old George Field, a neighbor who lived with his widowed mother.

George made an ideal hypnotic subject in that he readily went into a deep trance state. When regressed, many subjects are hazy about details. They cannot remember their full names or the names of their parents. They may not be certain where they lived and they are often unable to give other details that would be needed to check the validity of a story. Other subjects, although providing vivid details, describe an existence so long ago, or in so remote a place, that substantiation is out of the question. As Jonathan Powell, George Field was able to describe in great detail what appeared to be a previous existence. Of even greater importance was the fact that the past life which George Field recalled had been lived in North Carolina from 1832 to 1863, thus recent enough and close enough for extensive investigation.

"Are you going to let me hear what I said?" George Field asked.

"Sure," Williams answered, watching the spools of tape rewind. He had found that it never seemed to upset a subject to listen to himself recalling a presumed former life. Usually the subjects listened with a bemused kind of detachment, almost as if they were listening to an interesting radio program. Then, too, Williams always took the precaution to cut as briefly as possible, any traumatic experiences which the subject might recall. When an emotionally or physically painful episode was relived, the hypnotist would move the subject through the agony by jumping ahead in time or by easing the trauma through suggestion.

Williams punched a button on his tape recorder and once more the drama began to be played out. George Field had been conditioned through post-hypnotic suggestion to go into a deep trance state simply by Williams' saying, "Go to sleep, George." Thus, no time was lost in inducing hypnosis. Williams merely proceeded as follows:

"Go to sleep, George. I am going to count to three, and on the count of three I want you to go back to about the year 1840. On the count of three it will be the year 1840, and you will be deep asleep. One—two—three."

What are you doing?

Just sitting down.

Where are you?

In the woods.

What is your name?

Jonathan.

Jonathan, you can be wide awake now; your eyes will be wide open. You will be living as Jonathan about 1840. You will be able to remember things very clearly and you will be able to answer all my questions. You say that your name is Jonathan. Jonathan what?

Powell.

Jonathan Powell, I have a lot of questions for you, and I want you to answer them as best you can. What year is this?

1844.

How old are you?
Ten.
What month is this?
February.
Where do you live?
In Jefferson villie.
Jefferson?
Yes.
What state?
North Carolina.
What is your father's name?
Willard.
What does he do?
He plants a garden and sells some food and works up at the mine.
What is your mother's name?
I don't know.
Is your mother there?
No.
Where is she?
She died.
When?
I don't know.
Do you have any grandparents living, a grandmother or a grandfather?
No.
Do you remember what their names were?
My grandmother died last year. Her name was Mary.
Did she live with you?
No.
Where did she live?
Down the road.
How far?
Oh, about two miles.
Is that your father's mother or your mother's mother?
My father's mother.
So her name was Mary Powell?
Yes.

Where is your grandmother buried?
Down in the villie.
How far is it from the center of the village to your home?
About four or five miles.
In what direction?
That way. (Pointing)
Is that south or north or what?
It's that way. (Pointing again)
What does the land look like around your house?
It's fairly hilly; there's a hill over there.
A big one?
Good sized.
Are there any rivers or lakes around?
One river.
What is the name of that river?
I don't know. I go down there. Let's see, what do they call that? South Fork or something like that. Yes, South Fork, that's what it is.
Do you go swimming there?
Well, once.
How is it.
Well, it's okay. [As we shall learn, Jonathan may have had a good reason for not being enthusiastic about the water.]
Is it clean?
Yeah.
Do you have any brothers or sisters?
No.
Did you ever have any?
Not that I can remember.
How about any aunts or uncles, do you have any?
I've got an uncle, but he doesn't live around here.
Where does he live?
Way up North.
What is he, your mother's brother or your father's?
My father's brother.
What is his name?
It's Uncle Homer.
Did you ever see him?

No.

Do just you and your father live there on the farm?

Yes.

Where do you go to church?

It's up the road, up there.

Toward the village?

No, the other way.

Is it a big church?

No.

What does it look like?

Well, it's well, it looks like a church.

Has it got a big steeple on it?

No, no steeple. What's a steeple?

A big point on the top of it.

No.

What kind of a church is this?

It's the church that we go to. It's for Quakers like us.

So you are Quakers; are there many Quakers there?

Not too many.

How would you get to the church from the center of the village?

Well, you would go up the road that I live on, and it's about a mile from my house. It's just up there, you'll see it.

Is the cemetery near the church where your grandmother is buried?

No.

How about your mother, is she buried up there?

I don't know.

You said that your mother died. Do you remember your mother?

No.

I am going to count to three and you will go back to the day of your mother's funeral. You will remember what is going on and be able to tell me about it. One—two—three. Now what are you doing, Jonathan?

I'm at home.

How old are you?

Three.

Where is your father?
He's out back.
What is he doing?
I don't know.
Where is your mother?
I don't know where she is. (Crying)
Have you seen her?
(More crying, the tears of an anguished child.)
When did you see her last?
Yesterday.
What was she doing?
She—she went down to the villie.
Were you with her?
No.
Have you seen her since?
No.
Is she coming back?
Yes.
When?
I don't know.

I will count to three and it will be a month later, and then you can tell me about your mother. One—two—three. [This was done when Jonathan became so emotional that he could not be questioned further about that day.]

Where is your mother now, Jonathan?
Out back.
Where?
Out back of the house.
What is she doing?
Nothing.
What do you mean?
She's dead. (Crying)
Is she buried out there?
Yes.
Is there a little family cemetery there?
No.
Where is she buried, then?
Just out back.

Is there a gravestone for her?

No. Daddy just put up a cross.

What was the matter with your mother?

It happened down in the villie. She got run over out in the street by horses.

What was her name?

Marian.

Now, on the count of three, you will go back to the age of ten years old. One—two—three. We were talking about the church that you go to. Do you have a parson or minister there?

Don't know if he's a parson or not, but he tells us that we should do good, bah!

You don't believe all of it?

Well, most of it.

Where does he live?

Down in the villie somewhere. I don't know where.

How old is he?

Oh, he's pretty old.

What is his name?

Mr. Brown.

Does your father do anything besides work on the farm?

Yes, he works at the mine.

What mine?

It's about thirty miles away. They mine some kind of metal; tin, I think—I'm not sure.

Does he work there all year round?

No, they say it's pretty dangerous up there in the winter.

What town is this mine in?

I'm not sure. It's about thirty miles away. I've never been there.

How much money does he earn there?

He's never told me; but I don't think that he gets very much.

I will count to three now, and you will be twenty years old. One—two—three. How old are you now?

I'll be twenty tomorrow.

Do you still live on the farm with your father?

There's just me on the farm.
Where is your father?
He died.
When?
About three years ago. He got killed at the mine.
Where is he buried?
He's still in the mine.
Did it cave in?
Yes.
What do you raise on your farm?
I have some apple trees. I got some yams and some beans.
Have you ever been to the mine where your father
worked?
No.
Do you know what town it was in?
No.
I will count to three, and it will be January 1863. One
—two—three. What are you doing now, Jonathan?
I'm selling some stuff to some soldiers.
Where are the soldiers from?
The North.
What are you selling?
Some potatoes.
Where does the road go that you live on?
It goes over to the next state.
What state is that?
Tennessee.
How much is your farm worth?
Oh, it's not worth too much.
What could you sell it for?
*Oh, I guess I could sell if for ... well, two hundred and
fifty dollars easy.*
Do you still go to church every week?
Heck no, don't have time.
Who is the parson there now?
I wouldn't even know that.
Is Mr. Brown still alive, the one who used to preach there?
I'm not sure; he's a pretty old guy.

Have you gotten away from the Quaker religion, or have you just had no time?

Haven't had much time at all, boy.

Are you still interested in it?

Well, yeah, a little.

What do they believe in?

Well, the most important thing is that you shouldn't kill anyone or anything, not even if it tried to kill you. I've always gone by that.

How big a town is Jefferson?

Oh, heck, it must have at least three hundred people.

You call that a pretty big town, then?

Boy, I guess.

Are there any stores or businesses there in the village?

Well, there is the general store, but they don't sell too much there.

Who runs that?

Mr. Carter, I think. Yeah, that's him.

Is he an old fellow or a young fellow?

Well, I guess he's old. He's got white hair from here to yonder.

Are there any other businesses?

Well, there's, of course, the livery stable down there.

Who runs that?

I don't know that guy's name.

Any more businesses or stores?

Let me see. Well, I wouldn't call it a store, but Mrs. Abby down there, she sews for the women.

You sound as though you didn't have much use for the women.

Not for Mrs. Abby, I don't.

Why not?

Bah! All she does is yak, yak, yak!

That's women, isn't it?

Most of them, yes.

You never got married?

Heck no, not to a woman!

Is Jefferson on a main road?

A main road?

Yes, is it the main road from one important place to another?

Well, I guess you might call it a main road.

Where does it go besides Jefferson?

Well, besides Jefferson, do you mean the main road that goes through Jefferson, or the main road that goes out of Jefferson?

Well, both.

Oh, well, they hook on to each other up that way. I don't know where they go from there, but they hook on to each other.

What county is Jefferson in?

Ashe County.

Do you know any of the towns around there?

Well, I only know one, that's Clifton.

Do you vote in the elections?

Heck, no!

Don't you have anything to do with politics?

No! I stay away from those things.

I will count to three again and it will be your last day as Jonathan. One—two—three. What are you doing?

I'm loading the sacks of potatoes.

What are you loading them for?

For those damn Yankee soldiers.

Are they coming to buy some, or what?

Buy some! It's more like stealing them.

Why? Don't they pay you much?

No, I guess they don't. Here they come!

What do their uniforms look like?

They're gray.

They must be Southerners, then.

No, they ain't Southerners!

With gray uniforms?

Yes, sir.

How many potatoes do they want?

Five sacks, and they ain't getting them.

Why?

They pay ten cents! I don't want your money! Ten cents for my potatoes! OH! (Sounds of pain and coughing)

It's all right now. I will count to three and the pain will be gone. One—two—three.

What happened?

They shot me. (Crying)

Where did they hit you?

In the stomach. (Gasping and sobbing)

Does it hurt now?

A little.

Why did they shoot you?

I wouldn't take their damn money.

How do you feel now?

It still hurts a little.

Time will go on about five minutes on a count of three. One—two—three. Now what do you feel?

Nothing. I can't see anything. I can't feel anything.

On the count of three you will come back to the present time. One . . . two . . . three.

Very puzzled, George Field returned to his home that night after listening to the recording which he had made as "Jonathan." Was it possible, he had asked Williams, that he, a New England high school boy, had actually been that southern farmer? Was reincarnation really true or was it all crazy?

Although Loring G. Williams has had a lifelong interest in psychic phenomena and metaphysics, he, too, at the beginning of his research, had considered reincarnation to be "crazy." Williams had never been orthodox in his thinking, but reincarnation had always sounded kind of silly to him. It was one of those things that just was not, because everyone said that it could not be.

Then *The Search for Bridey Murphy* was published. It was shortly after his interest had been aroused by the controversy of the Bridey Murphy case that Williams attended a lecture at a psychical research society and observed a hypnotist regressing subjects to apparent former lives. The stories he heard that night sounded most convincing.

"But I didn't begin to practice and to study hypnosis in order to prove reincarnation," Williams is quick to point out. "After I had studied various kinds of psychic phenomena for a good many years, I became convinced that hypnosis could be the key to the subconscious and, at the same time, be used to control certain kinds of phenomena. It seems to me that these paranormal happenings are somehow controlled by definite physical laws. When we learn more about them we should be able to turn them on and off any time we want to."

Williams favors hypnosis rather than such chemical liberators of the subconscious as sodium pentothol because " . . . with drugs you get to the subconscious mind, but you lose control. In hypnosis, you have immediate control and you can turn it on or off at will—with absolutely no deleterious side effects. With drugs the researcher has the problem of proper supervision, the correct procedure of administration and the length of time that the drug would affect the subject and leave him groggy. Hypnosis is the natural answer all the way around."

Loring Williams' entire energy is continually channeled into a search for the best and most natural answers to life's questions. A graphoanalyst recently examined Williams' handwriting and declared him to be a mixture of the pragmatist and the idealist, the realist and the visionary.

Bill Williams has been a high school teacher for ten years. He holds a regular professional standard certificate and teaches electricity and industrial arts. A husky man who likes to "do for himself," Williams, as an avocation, remodels apartment buildings in his hometown, Hinsdale, New Hampshire. As good with his strong workman's hands as he is proficient at the art of hypnosis, forty-three-year-old Williams does all the labor himself, with the aid of his son Jack. Williams' wife Elsie, works at a local variety store. The Williamses' older son, Sherman, is a senior in college.

Bill Williams recalls that his father was interested in psychical research and undertook some experiments in mental healing. "He used to be a very good healer," Williams said. "I suppose that is one of the principal reasons why I became interested in hypnosis. I saw a way whereby I might be able to help people. Mental healing is a rare gift, but I reasoned that, as a hypnotist, I could deal directly with the subconscious mind and do more effective healing."

At one time Williams himself had the gift of touch healing. Just before he left for infantry training in World War II, he called on his fiancée, Elsie, and found her suffering from a chronic bronchial condition. She had contracted pneumonia as a baby and had been plagued with bronchial difficulties ever since.

"Elsie was in bed, so choked up that she could hardly breathe," Williams said. "I just put my hand on her forehead for about a minute, and all of a sudden, she sat up and said, 'I can breathe!' To this day she has never had a recurrence of the bronchial trouble."

Two years in the army, including about a year of service in Italy where he was chief radio operator for artillery headquarters, tended to make Williams a bit "rusty" as a touch healer. "I just didn't have any time to think for myself. From time to time I have been able to do a little touch healing since my army days, but not to the extent that I am certain I could have if I had seriously continued in the work."

After being discharged from the army, Williams worked as an electrician. For three years he was employed in the Portsmouth Naval Shipping yards, where he designed electrical systems for submarines. But it was in the field of teaching that Bill Williams felt he might best use his talents, and he left industry for the classroom and chalkboard ten years ago.

And now there was Jonathan Powell.

Williams knew that George Field had never had any particular interest in history or geography; and besides it would be out of the question that the historians of the Civil War would have digressed from accounts of Gettysburg, Vicksburg and Shiloh to detail the murder of a reclusive young North Carolina farmer. Jonathan Powell had been an ordinary man. No general on a charging white steed. No orator for the cause of freedom or apologist for slavery. Jonathan Powell had been a semiliterate, grumpy farmer who damn well minded his own business, thank you.

Before Williams became too excited about the search for Jonathan Powell, he made a trip to the library to look up the names of the towns and the county which Jonathan had mentioned. After all, to recite a list of names and places is one thing. To have them check out is quite another.

Williams' preliminary investigation established the geographical reality of Jefferson, *North* Carolina (Williams had asked the personality if he was certain that he had lived in North Carolina, because there is also a Jefferson, South Carolina. Jonathan became quite indignant at the question and said that he guessed he ought to know where he lived.) and the other geographical place names which Jonathan had mentioned. Williams resolved to begin making preparations for a trip to investigate the case of Jonathan Powell on the actual terrain where Jonathan claimed to have lived. George Field had not been the first subject whom Williams had regressed to an alleged former life, but he seemed to offer the greatest hope for firm substantiation.

Williams felt it was imperative George's story be recorded by a reputable group before a field trip was taken. That would allay the accusation, in case the search proved to be successful, that Williams had simply made up a story to fit any facts he found. Williams contacted Ted Mahoney, president of the Keene State College Psychical Research Society. Mahoney arranged a special meeting of the society at the home of Charles Cook, a clinical psychologist and president of the New Hampshire Psychic Research Society in Keene, New Hampshire.

On the agreed evening, George Field and Jack and Bill Williams drove to Cook's home. There were several people present, including Professor Charles Hapgood and Ted Mahoney. Recording equipment had been set up to make two tapes. One would be for Williams' further use in Jefferson, North Carolina, the other for the society's files.

Williams had prepared questions which he hoped would produce answers that could be checked against records in Jefferson. George Field had not been given any prior knowledge of these questions. In any questioning conducted during hypnotically induced regression, one cannot rigidly follow a planned outline. Changes are needed to explore any new information that may be forthcoming, and there is no point in pursuing a line of questioning in which the subject shows no interest. For example, Williams had spent some time looking up the names of the political figures in North Carolina during the 1800's, with the intention of questioning Jonathan about them; but it developed that the personality of the reclusive farmer had absolutely no interest in politics and did not read or write, or vote.

Williams did produce a bonus for the society, however. Under hypnosis, George Field recalled two additional lives (one as a girl) which led up to his incarnation as Jonathan Powell, a North Carolina farmer. Neither of the two pre-Jonathan lives offered any promise of possible substantiation, but the recording of Jonathan's birth experience is of special interest. Then, too, a pattern could be seen evolving in the linkup of lives between Chris-Janie-Jonathan-George that seemed to be saying something very important about the doctrine of reincarnation.

Hugh Roscoe, in his book *Occultism and Christianity*, presents a simple outline of reincarnation: " ... the Immortal Ego in man, that part which is divine, seeks expression in a succession of mortal physical bodies, with intervals of varying length spent on other planes of being between its incarnations."

Roscoe points out that the acceptance of the doctrine of reincarnation does not involve the assertion that all "Egos" came into the stream of spiritual evolution simultaneously; some souls are probably much older than others. "The philosopher may be conjectured to be an older soul than the society butterfly or the primitive savage."

The doctrine of reincarnation does imply, however, that
". . . at the start of their evolution, all souls had equal potentialities, and that their present positions represent exactly the
result of the use they have made of the time and opportunities
they had had so far."

Here, in an edited form, are the transcripts of the lives of
"Chris" and "Janie" and the birth of Jonathan Powell.

How old are you?

Fourteen.

What's your name?

Chris.

Do you have a last name?

I don't think so; they just call me Chris.

Where do you live?

I live down in the shipyards. I sleep in the outbuildings.

Do you have a mother and a father? (Chris shakes his
head negatively) You just live there alone?

Yes.

What do you do for food—do you work in the shipyards?

*Yes. We help splice the ropes and we help load on and
unload the spices.* [Williams produced a length of rope and
asked Chris to demonstrate his skill. Without hesitation, Chris
made a fast and expert splice. This is a work skill which lies
in the category of today's "lost arts" and is certainly beyond
the knowledge and dexterity of George Field.]

Do they pay you very much?

*They don't pay us at all; they just sometimes give us a
little.*

Do they give you any food?

Sometimes.

What do you do for food when they don't give you any?

Catch fish.

Where, off the pier there?

Yes.

Do you live with a lot of the other boys there?

One.

Who is he?

Bobby.

You don't go to school?

No.

Do you know what year this is?

I think it's 1628.

So you're fourteen years old and you just live around the shipyard. I'm going to count to three now and you will be twenty-five. One, two, three. Now what do you see?

Nothing. [The death experience had already taken place.]

I'll count to three then, and we'll go back to the time that you're twenty. One, two, three. Now what do you see?

Nothing.

I'll count to three, and we'll go back to your last day as Chris. One, two, three. Now what do you see?

A lot of men coming off the boat.

What are they doing? Working on the boat or sailing it?

They're unloading.

Where are you?

I'm at the dock.

Are you helping them or watching?

I'm watching them right now.

Now what is going on?

Ah! Ahhh! (Terrible screams and wild thrashing about)

What happened?

He pushed me in the water.

Can you swim?

No! (Frightened, gasping for breath)

Who pushed you?

A man.

Why?

I don't know. He was running. [Williams counts to three, removes the agony of drowning]

Did he push you by accident?

I guess so. [Williams moves Chris ahead in time a few minutes.]

Now what do you see?

Nothing!

What did you think about when you hit the water? Let's go

back a few seconds when you first go under water. One, two, three. Now what do you think?

Oh, get out! Must get out! [Williams moves him ahead once again to the first moments after death.]

Are you comfortable?

Yes.

What are you doing?

Nothing.

Can you see yourself now?

No.

Do you see anything around you?

No.

Do you see any lights, people or anything?

No.

What does it feel like you're doing?

Floating. [As we shall see, regressed subjects presumably recalling the moments after death often describe the sensation as "floating."]

Now I'm going to count to three again and you will go back another hundred years. It will be about 1500. One, two, three. Now what do you see?

Nothing much. Some trees.

Where are you?

I don't know. I don't know where it is. It's near the ocean.

How old are you?

Ten.

What's your name?

I don't know.

Are you a boy or a girl?

A girl.

You can speak up. You can open your eyes and see much better. Do you know what year this is?

No.

I'm going to count to three, and it will be one year later and things will be much clearer. One, two, three. Now what do you see?

I see people.

Do you know your name now?

Janie.

How old are you?

Eleven.

What's your last name?

I don't know.

Where are your mother and father?

I don't know.

Are they around there somewhere or haven't you seen them?

I haven't seen them.

How long has it been since you've seen them?

I've never seen them.

What do you do? How do you live?

Just walk around downtown.

Where do you get your food?

Steal it.

Where do you sleep?

Wherever I can. [Janie appears to have been one of those homeless street urchins who abounded in sixteenth century London.]

We'll go on to your last day as Janie. One, two, three. Now what do you see?

Aw! Oh! Ouch! Oh!

One, two, three, it will stop hurting. What happened?

A horse. A lot of horses. They didn't stop. I was on the street.

Where did they get you?

All over.

I'll count to three and it will stop hurting. Are you still lying on the street?

I can't see anything.

We will go back to about fifteen minutes before this happened. One, two, three. Now what do you see? What are you doing?

Just watching people.

Did you have anything to eat today?

No.

Did you have anything to eat yesterday?

Yes.
What did you have to eat yesterday?
Some dough.
Where did you get the dough?
Downtown. I stold it.
What do you have on for clothes?
Just plain old garb.
What's that?
Just some cloth.
Is it just wrapped around you or what?
It's just some clothes I stold from town.
Do you have any friends?
No.
No girl friend or no boy friends? Where do you live?
Anywhere.
Do you plan to steal all your life?
No. The horses! Here they come! No, no! Oh, Awhhh! [It is worth noting that Jonathan's *mother* allegedly suffered the same fate as Jonathan did in his previous life as Janie.]

One, two, three. Everything is all right now. Now you're going to go back farther and farther. Back to when you were four years old as Janie. One, two, three. Now what are you doing?
Just laying down.
Where?
On a board.
What board?
On the board I sleep on.
In your house?
Yes.
Who's with you?
I don't know.
How old are you?
Four.
Do you see anyone?
Yes, a friend.
What is he doing?
Lighting the fire.

Is it cold?
Not too cold.
What kind of a house is it?
Just a plain old house.
How big is it?
It's pretty big; it has two rooms.
Is there a woman there, too? (Janie shakes her head to indicate that there is not.) What do you call the man?
I don't.
Is he there all the time?
No.
Where do you get your food?
The guy.
But he doesn't live there?
No.
Who lives there?
A dog.
[Williams attempted to explore Janie's life in greater depth, but was unable to secure anything more than the most commonplace details of the life of an illiterate waif.

Williams then moved George Field ahead to 1845, and asked him what he saw. The reply was: *A garden.*]
Where is it?
In Jefferson villie.
How old are you?
Thirteen.
What's your name?
Jonathan Powell.
Is your mother or your father there?
Just my father.
Where's your mother?
She died.
When?
About four years ago.
What was her name?
Mary.
What's your father's name?
Willard.

Now I'm going to count to three, and you're going to go back to your first day as Jonathan. Tell me what you see. One, two, three.

They're looking at me.

Who?

The people.

Who are they? Do you know?

I'm not sure.

Have you ever seen them before?

No.

How old are you? How big are you?

I don't know. Not very big.

Where are you?

In bed.

What do you have on?

Nothing.

Do you see your mother?

I don't know who my mother is, but I see a lady.

You don't see her there?

Yeah, she's there! She's right there!

Who's the man? Is he your father?

I guess so.

All right, we're going to go back to the day before this. One, two, three! Now what do you see?

Nothing.

Where are you? What do you feel?

Nothing. Something jabbed me. Right there! [Could he be feeling the spasms of the approaching birth experience?]

Now what do you see?

It still isn't clear yet.

Let's go back about half an hour. One, two, three! Now what do you see?

Nothing. [But he goes on to complain at great length of being "jabbed in the bottom" and of being pulled and poked. Again, could he be describing the violent contractions of the womb and, perhaps, the assistance of a midwife or a doctor?]

Who's around you? Who do you see?

I don't see nothing.

We'll move along until you do see something. What do you see?

I don't know. Something's up there.

What do you mean, something's up there?

I don't know.

What are they? What do they look like?

They're big!

Do they look like people?

What's people?

Do you see yourself? Do they look something like you?

Something like me. But they're bigger.

What are these people doing there?

They're just standing up.

How many people are there?

Two.

Okay, we'll go on to a few more minutes, and you will be able to see things more clearly. One, two, three. What do you see?

Just the two people.

What are they doing?

They jabbed me. Don't jab me on the bottom!

Where is your mother?

She's jabbing me on the bottom!

You still have no clothes on?

Not very much. I see something white.

Now we'll go on to the next day. What do you see?

Those people over there.

Do you know who they are yet?

I think that they is my mommy and daddy.

Do they seem to like the looks of you very well?

I don't know. My mommy don't jab me on the bottom anymore.

Maybe you were bad.

I'm not doing anything.

I'm going to count to three, and it will be six months later. Now what are you doing?

On the floor. Just playing.

Who's around now?
No one.
Are you all alone? Where do you suppose they have all gone?
Outside.
What are you playing with?
Just with some little blocks.
Is it fun?
Yeah!

CHAPTER II

JONATHAN RETURNS TO JEFFERSON VILLAGE

Bill Williams was naturally eager to make his "psychic safari" to Jefferson, North Carolina, as soon as possible. It was decided that George Field, Williams and his son Jack would leave as soon as they could after the close of school. Since they would be traveling on a close budget, they decided to make it a camping trip.

Camping was a new experience for Williams, but the two boys had put in considerable tent time on camporees with the Boy Scouts. George had a tent that would sleep three, and Williams managed to round up three sleeping bags. A friend provided camp stoves. Finally, much to Elsie Williams' dismay, a pile of camping equipment began to collect on the dining room table.

Since they would be traveling by Volkswagen, a careful list of supplies had to be made and every unnecessary item eliminated. Williams considered it essential that they take along two tape recorders. First on the list was a large recorder on which to play the tape that had been made in Keene, and, if needed, to record any conversations which might be made in Jefferson that would be germane to the search for Jonathan Powell. The auxiliary tape recorder would be a small portable to use in the car.

Johnson City, Tennessee, lies only about sixty miles from Jefferson, North Carolina, and Bill Williams' old Army buddy, the Reverend Boyd E. Jackson, had a church in Watuga, Tennessee, just five miles east of Johnson City.

The Reverend Jackson and Bill Williams had been through the Italian campaign and had a good many old times to relive. Bill was not about to pass up an opportunity to renew an old and close friendship. Reverend Jackson willingly granted the Williams expedition tent space in the parsonage yard to use as a base of operations while they conducted research in Jefferson.

Thursday morning, after breakfast with the Jacksons, Williams and his two boys headed for Jefferson. Nestled in the mountains in the beautiful northwest corner of North Carolina, Jefferson, a village of 360 inhabitants, lies at the foot of Mount Jefferson. As he drove through the country-side, Bill Williams' memories were activated by the area's similarity to the Swiss Alps, where he had traveled extensive-ly after the war. But foremost in the researcher's thoughts was the knowledge that George Field had never been to North Carolina as George Field—yet here lay the Jefferson village countryside which Jonathan Powell had described so well. Would the irrefutable proof of reincarnation he sought be found in this tiny North Carolina village?

Williams' plan of operation on reaching Jefferson was to regress George Field to Jonathan Powell of 1860. He would then tour the town with him, study his reactions, and see what Jonathan recognized.

Williams felt hopeful. He had visions of Jonathan's leading them directly to his old house, finding his mother's grave in the backyard, and then going to the courthouse, where birth and death records of Jonathan, Willard, Mary, and Marian would be found. But things did not work out that way.

As they neared the village and came into view of Mt. Jefferson, which dominates the area, George Field claimed to have a definite feeling of having been there before. On entering the village, Williams told George to go to sleep and proceeded to regress him to 1860. Since they were riding in a car and would be meeting other cars, Williams had to tell Jonathan to pay no attention to the automobiles, which might have distracted or frightened him.

Jonathan was completely dismayed by the town. They

learned later that there are no buildings left in Jefferson which had been there a hundred years ago. The topography was familiar to Jonathan, but he could find no point from which to orient himself. He was aghast at the number and the size of the houses, and he was puzzled by what he called the "hard roads." At one point, when Williams stopped the car, Jonathan got out and jumped up and down on the pavement, trying to find out what had made it so hard.

Jonathan talked about the "big hill," Mt. Jefferson, and he knew that his house was near it; but changes in Jefferson so bewildered him that there was no hope of his locating his neighborhood.

The next step was to visit the Ashe County courthouse in Jefferson. There, Williams hoped to find birth and death records for Jonathan Powell and his family. Those hopes were shattered when Williams found that Ashe County had not maintained such records before 1912. This meant that if the existence of Jonathan or any members of his family were to be established, it would have to be done in some other way.

Williams explained their unique problem to John Gentry, the Registrar of Deeds for Ashe County. Williams then regressed George Field in an attempt to obtain details that might prove helpful. Gentry was amazed, but he was also very interested and most cooperative. He explained that while birth or death records had not been kept before 1912, there had been a registry of deeds since the formation of Ashe County, near the end of the eighteenth century.

Williams searched the old records of deeds and was excited to find, on page 430, Volume A, the copy of a deed in which in 1803 one Stephen Reed had conveyed to one Mary Powell a parcel of land. This information excited the researchers, because Jonathan had given the name Mary Powell as his grandmother's. The woman would have been of about the right age to be buying land in 1803; and, since Jonathan knew nothing about his grandfather, it could be assumed that Mary had been a widow for many years. In those days most of the women who bought land were either single or widowed.

Having found some record of "Grandmother Mary Powell," Williams tried to determine what had become of the parcel of land. He hoped to find a record to show that it had been deeded to Willard, and subsequently to Jonathan. But once again the hypnotist came to a dead end. A search of the registry failed to show that Mary Powell had ever disposed of this land by deed.

Mr. Gentry then took them to the probate office, but a search there showed no record that Mary Powell had ever bequeathed the land or that it was ever transferred by probate court order. On the records, the land seemed to have disappeared. It was explained to Williams that this was not unusual, because many land transfers were not recorded and when a parcel of land was sold the seller sometimes merely endorsed the deed over to the new owner. When a landowner died his family just continued to live on the property, with no record of transfer or probate.

Williams considered it significant, however, that they had found Mary Powell, especially in view of their later ascertaining that Powell had not been a name common in the area. They did find a record of one other Powell, but could not connect him to either Jonathan or Mary.

Mr. Gentry also referred Williams to a local historian who had undertaken to establish the genealogies of all the old families of Ashe County. She would be familiar with names of persons who had lived in Jefferson and the surrounding area during Jonathan's time.

Williams called her and made an appointment for that afternoon. When they arrived at her home Williams explained that this would probably be the strangest case in which she would ever be called upon for assistance. The historian agreed that she was not accustomed to entertaining people who claimed to have lived in Jefferson over a hundred years ago. She expressed herself most emphatically that she did not believe in "this sort of thing," but, nevertheless, she consented to help all she could. This attitude, from Williams' point of view, was good. No one could claim that the historian was prejudiced in their favor.

Williams played the duplicate tape made at the meeting of the New Hampshire Psychic Research Society so that she might become familiar with Jonathan's background. Williams then regressed George to Jonathan in 1860 so he could be questioned about Jefferson. Williams chose the year 1860 because that was the latter part of Jonathan's life, when he should have had the broadest knowledge of the town and its inhabitants.

After she heard the Keene tape, the historian conceded amazement at Jonathan's knowledge of Jefferson, but was still skeptical. Once Williams had regressed George Field, however, the historian proceeded to question him about people and events of 1860 and before. Williams cautioned her to keep the questions in the present tense, because as far as Jonathan was concerned it *was* 1860.

Historian: (Again expressing reluctance) I don't know if I should do this . . . (nervous chuckle).

Williams: Okay, George, I'm going to take you back to 1860 when you were Jonathan. You will be wide awake, and there is someone here who wants to ask you some questions about the town. It is 1860, and now you're Jonathan.

Historian: Jonathan, remember Joshua Baker when he was high sheriff of Ashe?

Jonathan: I think that it was about ten years ago that he was sheriff. I don't know I've ever met him or anything, but I think it was about ten years ago that he was there.

(*A fact. Joshua Baker had been high sheriff about 1850, "ten years ago" from 1860.*)

Historian: Do you know anything of Whispering Jim Dixon?

Jonathan: No.

Historian: You never heard of him, and you don't know why they called him Whispering Jim?

Jonathan: No.

Historian: It was because he talked loud. He was a well-to-do man. *(This may explain why Jonathan Powell did not know him. A small acreage farmer would not necessarily be acquainted with the village elite. Still, it seems that Jonathan might at least have heard of him.)*

Historian: Do you know about the drowning of Colonel George Bower?

Jonathan: No. *(The historian later recalled that Colonel Bower had drowned in 1863 or '64. Jonathan had been sent back to 1860 and so could not have known of the Colonel's fatal accident, which was still in the future.)*

Historian: What do you know about the attitude the slaves had in Ashe County after they were freed?

Williams: (Reminding the historian to phrase her questions circa 1860.) He was killed before that time.

Historian: Where were you born, Jonathan?

Jonathan: Well, I was born up there in Jefferson.

Historian: Right in the town of Jefferson?

Jonathan: Yeah, at our house.

Historian: Just whereabouts is your house located from the courthouse?

Jonathan: Facing the big hill.

Historian: And that's what we call Negro Mountain.

Jonathan: (Not familiar with the historian's name for the "big hill.") It was right on the hillside, facing the big hill.

Historian: Were you personally acquainted with Patten Colvers?

Jonathan: I've heard of him, but I've never met him. I know I've heard of him.

Historian: Do you recall hearing about a stone rolling out of the mountains the day one of his daughters was born?

Jonathan: No, I never heard about that.

Historian: Were you acquainted with the rich merchant Wall?

Jonathan: No.

Historian: You knew none of the Walls?

Jonathan: There was a Samuel Wall. I knew him.

Historian: All right, Samuel Wall lived in Jefferson at that time; but you didn't know the rich old merchant?

Jonathan: I didn't know him. (*This is fairly significant. Jonathan could easily have said that he knew the "rich merchant Wall." Instead, Jonathan said that he knew Samuel Wall, who also lived in Jefferson at that time.*)

Historian: Were you acquainted with David Worth?

Jonathan: Let's see, David Worth. . . . I think he lived down in the center of the villie. We don't get down there too much. Yeah, I know he lives there. But I've never met him. (*Although Jonathan said he did not know David Worth, the historian conceded that he had accurately placed Worth's residence in Jefferson.*)

Historian: What have you heard of the Perkins family?

Jonathan: What do you mean, what have I *heard* of them?

Historian: Have you heard anything of them and what they did before 18 and 60?

Jonathan: No.

Williams: Do you know any of the Perkinses, Jonathan?

Jonathan: (A bit impatiently) No.

Historian: Did you know Jonathan Baker?

Jonathan: Yeah, he lived down in the center of the villie, too. I've met him quite a few times, and I've seen him down there. He's got quite a bit of money, I think! And he always talks about it too! I think he's got quite a few slaves. (*The historian chuckled and nodded throughout Jonathan's enthusiastic recounting of the wealth of Jonathan Baker. Obviously Jonathan Powell had provided a good deal of correct information about Jonathan Baker.*)

Historian: What do you know about James Baker?

Jonathan: Not much, not too much.

Historian: Do you recall Thomas Callaway?

Jonathan: No.

Historian: I don't know how you could have missed him.

Jonathan: Why?

Historian: Well, he was a prominent man and was around Jefferson a lot. What about the Ray family? Do you recall meeting any members of the Ray family?

Jonathan: Let's see . . . there was a girl. She was about my age, too. I think her name was Mary.

Historian: And she never married?

Jonathan: No, I don't think so.

Historian: (Chuckling) Aunt Polly.

Jonathan: Who's Aunt Polly?

Historian: Aunt Polly was Mary Ray. Her nickname was Aunt Polly. (*This is a solid hit. Jonathan seemed to know the Ray family quite well, for he became excited at the mention of their name. In 1860, Mary Ray would have been just Jonathan's age. The fact that he is unfamiliar with the "Aunt Polly" nickname is hardly surprising. "Aunt" is a common name given to spinsters in the South, but Mary Ray would not really have been old enough to have given up hope of marriage at the time of Jonathan's death. Mary Ray, or "Aunt Polly," was a well-known member of the historian's family, and Jonathan's knowledge of her seemed to satisfy the historian that she had not really embarked on a foolish chore. For those who will instantly seize upon this fact and attempt to convert it to proof of Jonathan's reincarnation being but a manifestation of "psi" ability (i.e., that he "picked" the knowledge of Mary Ray from the historian's subconscious), one must immediately ask why Jonathan did not also "get" the "Aunt Polly" nickname. Then, too, if George Field were but a brilliant clairvoyant and actor, why should he "recall" some names and miss others? To make his performance look more convincing? This argument would hardly seem to hold, for if one were out to hoax, the more perfect the score the better one would be able to deceive the gullible into accepting "proof" of reincarnation.*)

Historian: When you were out in the Ore Knob section in the copper mine. . . .

Williams: (Interrupting her) He was never at the mine. He doesn't even know for sure where it was. Do you know now where that mine is where your father worked, Jonathan?

Jonathan: No, I just know that it's north of here. I don't know where it is. (*Again, if this were all clairvoyance, it would seem that George-Jonathan's entering into rapport with the historian would have enabled him to be precise about the location of the mine. From the first hypnotic session Jonathan had openly professed his ignorance of the mining area.)*

Historian: You have no memory of the Reeves family being connected with the mine?

Jonathan: Reeves ... Thomas Reeves? My father spoke of him. Yeah, he spoke of him often, but I don't remember what for. ...

Historian: You never heard of Alexander or Charles?

Jonathan: Ah ... Alexander, I think. He lived not too far from our house. Boy, was he rich! Oh, I guess! *(Although Jonathan knew nothing of the mining area, he seemed to have rather clear memories of his father's discussions of his employers.)*

Historian: Do you remember the Koontz family?

Jonathan: Koontz? No.

Historian: John and George Koontz? What about the Lewis family? Do you remember Gideon Lewis or Isaac Lewis?

Jonathan: (Becoming excited) Isaac! Yeah, yeah, he lives down the road from me about a mile or so. I don't know his wife, but I do know Isaac! He's come up to see me before! *(A solid hit. Jonathan apparently knew Isaac Lewis, where he lived, his profession and his marital state. Isaac Lewis must have been one of the few neighbors that the reclusive Jonathan then received as a visitor. The fact that Jonathan did not know Isaac's wife should not surprise us. Remember that the young farmer has never attempted to conceal his misogyny.)*

Historian: Do you remember James McMullen? James or John McMullen?

Jonathan: I remember Tom McMullen. I don't know if he's related to James or John, but I know Tom. *(Not conclusive. The historian was uncertain whether Tom McMullen had existed or not.)*

Historian: Do you know Douglas Dickson?

Jonathan: I don't *know* him, but I've heard of him. Everyone speaks of him. I don't know what for, but they all talk about him.

Historian: No doubt you were acquainted with James Eller.

Jonathan: Not personally acquainted, but I've seen him.

Historian: What does he look like?

Jonathan: Well, he's fairly tall, and he has black hair. I think that's all you can tell. I never looked closely at his eyes or anything, but I think they're brown.

Historian: You should get better acquainted with him.

Jonathan: (In a rather indifferent tone) Why?

Historian: He's a leading citizen.

Jonathan: He is? I've heard a lot talked about him, but I've just seen him. I've never met him. *(This would seem to be a hit in that Jonathan definitely seems to know something about James Eller. If one should find it a bit strange that in a village as small as Jefferson, Jonathan knows so few people personally, he should be reminded that Jonathan was basically something of a loner, who cared not at all for the society of women, and little for the company of men. Jonathan would have been the sort to withdraw from the leading citizens with whom the historian admonishes him to "get better acquainted.")*

Historian: Have you met Drury Center?

Jonathan: Who?

Historian: Drury or Nathaniel Center.

Jonathan: No, but I heard about them, too.

Historian: They were both prominent. Our Baptist church is named after them.

Jonathan: I don't go to a Baptist church!

Historian: Well, you should know about them. *(But Jonathan did say he had heard of the Centers. There seems little reason for a Quaker to have become particularly well-acquainted with the Baptist clergy. And, in 1860, Jonathan surely would not be aware that the Baptists would one day name a church in honor of Drury and Nathaniel Center.)*

Historian: You know about Francis Asberry, don't you?

Jonathan: No, who's he?

Historian: He came through this section just before the year 18 and 60.

Jonathan: What he come through here for?

Historian: Well, he was a minister and he wanted to lead us to Christ. That's what all ministers are supposed to do.

Jonathan: Well, I don't want to go there yet! *(Again we must take into account that the young farmer has abandoned "churchgoing" at this point in his life. It is not really so strange that he would not be aware of Reverend Asberry's visit.)*

Historian: Do you recall meeting Steven Thomas shortly after he moved to this county from the state of Virginia?

Jonathan: I've never met him, but I saw him getting his pants mended at Mrs. Abby's one time!

Historian: What kind of house did Mrs. Abby live in?

Jonathan: Not a very good one, but it was better than mine.

Historian: You probably remember when Colonel Bower built his brick home in Jefferson?

Jonathan: Yeah, I think it was about ten or twelve years ago. It was in the 1840's. *(A good hit. The Bower home was built in 1848. Since Jonathan is speaking from the year 1860, his "ten or twelve years" hits the date right on the nose!)*

Historian: Do you remember meeting his wife?

Jonathan: No, I stay away from girls!

Historian: Do you remember going to the courthouse and having any deeds recorded when Robert Gamble was registrar?

Jonathan: No, I never been in the courthouse.

Historian: You've never been in the courthouse?

Jonathan: No.

Since the historian's interview of Jonathan Powell was much more than a yes or no quiz, it is impossible to provide the odds on his hits and misses. The historian asked Jonathan about a total of twenty-five persons or events in Jefferson circa the year 1860. Jonathan readily admitted having no knowledge of some of them, but he did claim to know something about fifteen of the individuals and items on which he was queried. Over fifty percent of his "hits" mentioned such correct details as financial status, physical descriptions, children's names, location of residences and the construction of homes. On one hand, it would be correct to say that George Field should have known *no* details about Jefferson "villie," North Carolina, in 1860. At the same time, he could have answered yes to every question. The fact that he offers correct details in his answers rules out the possibility of guessing. His misses only prove that Jonathan, the reclusive young farmer, did not know everyone in Jefferson. In Williams' opinion, Jonathan gave enough detailed responses to make the possibility of chance very remote.

One of the principal objects of Williams' search was the mine in which Willard Powell was supposed to have been killed. The best known mine in the area is the Ore Knob, a copper mine about ten miles out of Jefferson. The historian knew that there had been a cave-in there at one time and checked it out for Williams. She found that the period of greatest activity at the Ore Knob mine was in the 1870's and that the cave-in had occurred after the Civil War. She had obtained the names of the men who were killed in the cave-in and Willard Powell was not among them.

Williams did learn, however, that in that area there had been many small mines in operation over the past 150 years, many of them one and two man operations of which there are no present records. The researchers could neither prove nor disprove that Willard Powell was killed in a mine cave-in.

They replayed the tape they had made on the preceding day to get the historian's reaction once again to Jonathan's answers. To Williams it seemed amazing and very significant that one who had never had any connection with Jefferson could know so much about the village.

A point of interest was the church that Jonathan claimed to have attended. The historian knew nothing of a Quaker church in the area, but she did know that the Mr. Brown of whom Jonathan had spoken was a sort of circuit-riding preacher who often came through Jefferson.

Williams seemed to have exhausted whatever information there was to be obtained from the historian. However, he did have other experiences during the stay in and about Jefferson.

When they were riding around town with George regressed to Jonathan they drove through West Jefferson, which is about two miles from Jefferson proper. There Jonathan did not recognize the topography. Williams told him that they were in West Jefferson, but he insisted that there was no such place, only Jefferson. This seemed strange to Williams, but he found out later that West Jefferson was not settled until after 1900, and so, of course, Jonathan was right!

Another interesting and humorous episode was their experience with snuff. In New Hampshire today, snuff is practically unheard of. But one day while Williams and the boys were driving to Jefferson they heard on the car radio an advertisement for snuff. The boys had never heard of it, but Williams had worked in the South and had seen snuff used, so he explained to them what little he knew about it.

Later that day, Williams went into a supermarket in Jefferson to pick up food for their lunch. There he noticed a large display of snuff and purchased a can as a souvenir for the boys.

After lunch, as they were riding around Jefferson with George, regressed to Jonathan, in an attempt to locate his farm, Williams happened to think of the snuff and asked Jonathan if he liked it. He said that he "sure did." Williams gave him the can. He had trouble getting it open because he had never seen that kind of "new-fangled" box before. Jack Williams had to open it for him. Jonathan then proceeded to blow into the box in an apparently accustomed manner. Forming it into a cloud, he snuffed it up his nose. Williams had never seen snuff used in this manner, but he remembered from an article he had read about snuff that this was the popular way to use snuff years ago in that section of the country. It would be difficult to believe that anyone could accomplish it as expertly as Jonathan did, without practice. Williams knew that George Field had never seen this done, nor had he ever had any previous experience with snuff.

The final phase of Williams' adventure into Jonathan Powell's past is the evaluation of his findings. Williams has tried to remain objective and to maintain a scientific approach. This, however, has been a bit difficult at times, because Jonathan has become like a member of his family.

Probably the best approach is to compare Jonathan's claims, recorded on the Keene tape, against what was found to be true and untrue. In evaluating information of this sort one must always bear in mind that lack of proof does not in itself disprove anything.

The tape established a Jonathan Powell as living in Jefferson, North Carolina, in 1844. The existence of the town of Jefferson is a fact, but the existence of Jonathan was not established by any official record. Williams considers it to be of some significance that George Field would name such a town as Jefferson. It is a small village in a remote western section of North Carolina. It is highly improbable that George had ever heard of it. Most people from their section of New Hampshire who have occasion to travel through North Carolina do so on the way to Florida. Such travelers usually use routes 1, 301 or 17, all of which take them far to the east of Jefferson. Jonathan also said that Jefferson was located in Ashe County, which is correct.

The tape named Jonathan's father as Willard Powell, and said that he did a little farming and worked in a mine. No record of Willard was found, but there were many small mines in the area and it is more than likely that a laborer living in Jefferson at that time would on occasion work in a mine.

Mining is not the sort of occupation a New Hampshire boy would normally think of for his father. Another interesting point is that none of the reference books that Williams had available mentioned mining in the Jefferson area.

The tape established Jonathan's grandmother as Mary Powell, who died prior to 1843 and had been buried in the village. Williams' search of the Jefferson registry showed that a Mary Powell had bought land in 1803. This would establish her at about the right age to have been Jonathan's grandmother. The fact that Powell was not a common name in Jefferson's history makes the discovery of Mary even more significant.

The researchers were unable to locate Mary's grave. Only a small section of the Jefferson cemetery dates to the time of Mary Powell's death, and many of the old stones are weathered and illegible. Jonathan insisted that it was not the cemetery where his grandmother was buried, and Williams later found that there had been another, earlier cemetery in a different section of town. Williams and the boys did not visit this graveyard because they were told that no legible stones remained there.

Jonathan said that the land around his house was hilly with "a good-sized hill over there." The surrounding countryside is very mountainous and Jefferson is on a rolling valley. The "good-sized hill over there" could be Mt. Jefferson, which rises sharply from the valley to dominate the area.

On the tape, Jonathan described a river called South Fork. Williams and the boys found that the New River branches into South Fork and North Fork. South Fork runs near Jefferson. This is a very significant item, because the maps that Williams had available for preliminary investigation in New Hampshire did not name this stream. It is difficult to see how George Field could have learned that there was a South Fork River near Jefferson.

Jonathan named Clifton as the town next to Jefferson. This is true.

Also, on the tape Jonathan mentioned the church which he claims to have attended. This church was not the Baptist Church in the center of town, but was apparently four or five miles out in the country. When Williams asked him about a steeple, Jonathan did not know what one was. Most of the early churches (and many today in that section of the country) had no steeples. Williams found no record of this church or of there having been Quakers in the area. Jonathan, of course, had said that there were only a few of them.

Jonathan tells that his mother was buried out behind his house with only a cross for a grave marker. This was common practice throughout the country at that time. He remembers that the minister who conducted the services at the church was a Mr. Brown. The researchers found that a Mr. Brown had been a sort of circuit-riding preacher in the area at the time Jonathan claimed to have known him.

He mentioned Mr. Carter's store and Mrs. Abby. Williams found no record of the store, but there had been Carters in the area at the time; and, according to Jonathan, the store was small and did little business. Williams also learned that there had been a family named Abby living in Jefferson at the time.

Perhaps the most significant part of the tape is the description of Jonathan's death. The young farmer claimed that in 1863 he was shot by Yankee soldiers because he would not sell them his potatoes for ten cents a bushel. Jonathan stated that these soldiers wore gray uniforms but that they were not Confederate soldiers. As far as any Civil War records that Williams could find were concerned, there were no Yankee troops in North Carolina in 1863, and even the most casual student of American history knows that the North wore blue, not gray, uniforms.

Again, uncovered bits of random information proved that Jonathan might have been correct. The local historian told Williams that at the time there were bands of renegades who came down from the North, usually from Kentucky, using the war as an excuse to raid and plunder. These renegades could well have been dressed in gray, because it would not be unthinkable for them to have murdered a small band of Confederate soldiers and stolen their uniforms.

Shortly after the article by Williams describing the rebirth of Jonathan Powell appeared in *Fate* magazine, George Field received further substantiation of Jonathan Powell's existence in a letter from a woman whose maiden name had been Powell and who claimed to be a greatniece of Jonathan's. The woman went on to clear up a number of items which, according to her recollection, were incorrectly stated by the personality of Jonathan.

"Jonathan Powell was my great-uncle. He was killed by the

Yankees, so my father said; but [my father] didn't know any details at all. Willard Powell was Jonathan's brother. Jim Powell was Jonathan's father [it appears that Jonathan may have switched names and forgotten a brother]—and he was redheaded, or sandy haired, and all the family had blue eyes. We never knew what became of Willard or his family.

"There is West Jefferson and Old Jefferson, and Old Jefferson is three miles from there. . . .

"My mother often talked about the Quakers, and they would spend the night with her family over there.

"Jim Powell was not killed in the mines. It could have been Willard [which could have set up Jonathan's identification of the name "Willard" with his father instead of with his brother].

"I haven't done any research on history, but a lot of those eastern Tennessee men fought for the South. That could have been some of them in the gray uniforms who killed Jonathan, or it could have been the renegades."

Lafcadio Hearn observed that for thousands of years the East has been teaching that what we think or do in life really determines the future place and state of our essential substance. "Acts and thoughts, according to Buddhist doctrines, are creative," Hearn writes in *Kotto*. "What we think or do is never for the moment only, but for measureless time; it signifies some force directed to the shaping of worlds—to the making of future bliss or pain."

Reincarnation is an ancient doctrine, ancient even at the time of the Greek and Roman Empires. Plotinus, in the *Second Ennead*, writes that reincarnation is " . . . a dogma recognized throughout antiquity . . . the soul expiates its sins in the darkness of the infernal regions, and . . . afterwards . . . passes into new bodies, there to undergo new trials."

The Koran, holy book of the Moslem faith, states that ". . . God generates beings and sends them back over and over again, til they return to Him."

St. Augustine asks the eternal question in his *Confessions*: "Say, Lord, to me . . . say, did my infancy succeed another age of mine that died before it? Was it that which I spent within my mother's womb? ... and what before that life again, O God, my joy, was I anywhere or in any body?"

Benjamin Franklin pragmatically saw the whole thing as a simple matter of economy. "When I see nothing annihilated [in the works of God] and not a drop of water wasted, I cannot suspect the annihilation of souls, or believe that He will suffer the daily waste of millions of minds readymade that now exist, and put Himself to the continual trouble of making new ones. Thus, finding myself to exist in the world, I believe I shall ... always exist; and, with all the inconveniences human life is liable to, I shall not object to a new edition of mine, hoping, however, that the *errata* of the last may be corrected."

The quick wit of Voltaire expressed the mystery of reincarnation succinctly when he said: "It is not more surprising to be born twice than once; everything in Nature is resurrection."

Whether or not the case of George Field-Jonathan Powell establishes the truth of reincarnation must, perhaps, remain a question each reader will have to decide for himself. The skeptic will probably feel that nothing has been proven—that there are no facts, only a few coincidences. The believer will proclaim that at last we have been given absolute proof of reincarnation.

Loring Williams is convinced that Jonathan Powell did live in Jefferson, North Carolina, from 1834 to 1863. After having met Jonathan through George Field, and visiting Jefferson with him, Williams says he can believe nothing else.

In *Religion and Immortality*, Professor G. Lowes Dickinson expressed his view that reincarnation offered a " ... really consoling idea that our present capacities are determined by our previous actions, and that our present actions again will determine our future character." Such a philosophy, Professor Dickinson observes, liberates man from the bonds of an external fate and makes him the captain of his own destiny.

"If we have formed here a beatuiful relation, it will not

perish at death, but be perpetuated, albeit unconsciously, in some future life. If we have developed a faculty here, it will not be destroyed, but will be the starting point of later developments. Again, if we suffer ... from imperfections and misfortunes, it would be consoling to believe that these were punishments of our own acts in the past, not mere effects of the acts of other people, or of an indifferent nature over which we have no control."

In the hypothesis of reincarnation, Professor Dickinson remarks, the world would at least seem to be more just than it is in the positivist view, " ... and that in itself would be a great gain."

CHAPTER III

HOW MANY PEOPLE ARE YOU?

In 1964, Dr. Samuel Morris, a Jerusalem dental surgeon, made the astonishing discovery that he had a son who was three years old in body and 3,000 years old in spirit.

Dr. Morris's wife, Edna, had complained that their son, David, had been walking about the house speaking in gibberish. The boy seemed normal enough when he was around other children and when Dr. Morris came home from work, but Mrs. Morris was becoming increasingly irritated by her son's strange behavior.

"He may be doing it just to annoy me," she said to her husband. "I want you to arrange an appointment with a child psychologist."

Dr. Morris complied with his wife's wishes and arranged for a consultation with a psychologist. When he went home to pick up his son, Dr. Morris found the boy building a fortress out of blocks. The strange design seemed oddly familiar. Dr. Morris puzzled over the configuration for a few moments and then it struck him. His three-year-old son had constructed a scaled-down model of a holy temple of which Dr. Morris had seen archaeologists' drawings during a tour of the National Museum just a few weeks before. But David had not seen the exhibit and had never been inside the museum.

When Dr. Morris asked his son what he had built, David answered in the nonsense words that had so irritated Mrs. Morris. As fast as the words poured from the boy's lips, Dr.

Morris was able to understand only a few—principally *mikdash*, the Hebrew word for temple.

When Dr. Morris played a tape recording of his son's babblings for Dr. Zvi Hermann, acting curator of the ancient manuscripts section of the National Museum, the scholar pronounced the words to be ancient Hebrew. Dr. Hermann explained that most words spoken today in Israel are the same as the ancient language, but " ... the inflection, accent and grammar are vastly different."

After listening to the tape recording a number of times, Dr. Hermann translated the message as that of a king exhorting his followers to rally about him so that he might lead them to glory. In the Hebrew scholar's opinion, the tape sounded like a professional actor rehearsing a role in a play. He was especially reminded of King David's struggle against the faction which had opposed the construction of the temple in Jerusalem. Powerful opposition had forced King David to abandon the project before its completion, but King Solomon, his successor, had finished the task.

"I had no idea such a play had been written," Dr. Hermann remarked. "It makes an excellent subject for drama. And I had no idea that any of our actors knew ancient Hebrew. This young man is brilliant! I have yet to meet anyone who speaks the old language as fluently as he does. Who is he?"

"My three-year-old son, David," Dr. Morris replied softly.

In the January 1968 issue of *Fate* Magazine, Leo Heiman reports his investigation and analysis of the boy, now nearly seven, who speaks in the voice of the mighty King David of Jerusalem, who lived 3,000 years ago.

Dr. Morris told Heiman that he had never believed in reincarnation and had considered it utter nonsense. "As a medically and scientifically trained person I was a materialist, an agnostic, who doubted even the existence of God, let alone supernatural occurrences. But this is a case in which the facts speak for themselves. ... "

Psychologists have reported that young David Morris is normal in his behavior when the windows of his room are

kept shut, but slips into trance when they are open. They
have also determined that the trances are most frequent
when the wind blows from the northeast, the direction in
which lies the site of King David's original fortress.

Dr. Morris took his son, Dr. Hermann and a tape recorder
to the tomb of King David. As they began to climb the 188
stone steps which lead to the tomb, David Morris fell into a
trance which lasted for twenty minutes. Dr. Hermann translated the boy's speech in the presence of two other scholars
who specialized in the study of ancient Hebrew. "King David's" words concerned themselves with a command to seize
Jerusalem from the infidels and a protest against the com-
mercialization of the tomb.

Dr. Hermann counseled Dr. Morris in a serious manner
after he had deciphered a number of "King David's"
speeches. It seemed to him that three things would happen if
they were to give the case any publicity. They would probably all be committed to institutions for psychiatric examina-
tions and therapy. They would be accused of warmongering
and of exploiting a child for purposes of nationalist propa-
ganda that emphasized destroying the infidels "with fire and
sword." Religious groups would descend upon them because
their dogma maintained that King David's soul was in heav-
en, not reincarnated in the person of a young boy.

A vacation trip in the summer of 1966, which had been
designed to exorcise the spirit of King David, ended in
anguish. At the Parthenon on Acropolis Hill in Athens, David
thundered at his parents for taking him to "pagan temples
with graven images of their stupid little gods"! The boy
refused to eat and spent most of his time weeping. Within
two weeks the Morris family returned to Jerusalem, resolved
to ignore the boy's trances.

A child psychologist interpreted David Morris's "problem"
as an imaginative identification with King David. He advised
Dr. Morris to encourage his boy to begin drawing, singing
and playing musical instruments. Since King David had done
these things, the psychologist argued, the Morrises might as

well capitalize on the boy's identification by encouraging him
in creative pursuits.

"But how can the boy imagine himself to be King David
when he does not yet know who King David was?" Dr.
Morris wanted to know.

The psychologist refused to accept the suggestion that
David Morris had made anything more than a subconscious
identification with the monarch of ancient Israel's Golden
Age.

Dr. Morris did heed the psychologist's advice, however,
and brought David to a music teacher. The boy quickly
demonstrated musical ability but showed little interest in any
of the instruments. Then one day David was shown a harp.
Although he had never held such an instrument before, the
five-year-old lad plucked at the strings and produced a
strange, lilting melody, with a rhythm and melody line unknown to the teacher or to any musician or scholar who
subsequently heard the boy play. The harp, of course, was
the instrument King David had played from his days as a
shepherd boy.

On May 15, 1967, while Israel celebrated the nineteenth
anniversary of her independence with fireworks, music and
dancing, little David Morris sat in silence for a long time,
then begged his father to take him to Mount Zion. There, at
the tomb of King David, the boy predicted the six-day war
with the four Arab nations which would soon begin.

"Do not despair," David reassured his father, "victory will
be ours. The Lord shall lead us to victory. Have faith!"

On June 26, Dr. Morris, just home from the Medical
Corps, left on a much different expedition. Leading a proces-
sion which made its way along the Valley of the Ghosts
toward the walls of Old Jerusalem was six-year-old David
deep in trance. The remainder of the company was composed
of Dr. Hermann, two archaeology students, and reporter
Heiman. King David had promised to show them how he
seized the city of Ur Salim (Jerusalem) and took it from his
Canaanite enemies.

The ancient military coup has long been hotly debated by

historians. One school of thought holds that David and a handful of carefully selected men stormed the cliffs of Mount Moriah to besiege the city. Other historians contend that the monarch found a secret passageway in the fortress and seized the city with a small band of commandos.

In the Cave of Gichon the boy led the way to a pile of boulders. He pointed upward. "There is the way!"

Reporter Heiman could see nothing, but one of the students investigated and discovered a narrow shaft. The next day a group of archaeology students, led by twenty-four-year-old Moshe Lerer, climbed up the passageway and emerged, 549 feet up, in the central courtyard of El Omar Mosque on Mount Moriah.

Heiman writes that " . . . heated arguments between scholars still are raging in the popular and professional press as to whether this secret passage was used by King David and his commando raiders or whether the shaft was used only by subsequent conquerors who sacked the Holy City."

Because he was there, journalist Heiman knows that six-year-old David Morris had led the way to a cave he had never seen or heard of and pointed out a shaft that no in the party knew existed.

The archaeological students drew detailed plans of the secret passageway which illustrated that it connects at an intermediate level with one of Mount Moriah's water wells. The water in this part of the passage is only hip deep, and man-made foot and hand holds gouged into the rock thousands of years ago await the traveler at another opening.

The ambitious and enthusiastic students made the climb again, timing their progress with stopwatches. According to Moshe Lerer, " . . . it is the best, quickest and most efficient way of seizing an impregnable mountaintop fortress. I am sure King David conquered Ur Salim this way."

Is David Morris the reincarnation of King David? How did he know of the secret passageway into the Old City, and from what source does he make predictions of another war against the "infidels"?

According to Heiman, the boy warns of continued conflict

with the "godless tribes of Amalek, Moab and Edom." He does not mention Arabs, because they did not inhabit the Holy Land in King David's time. But, Heiman points out, "The map shows the Amalekite Hills in Egyptian territory, the mountains of Moab and Edom in Trans-Jordan and southern Syria."

Rabbi Yedidia Cohen of the Supreme Religious Council was quoted by reporter Heiman on the strange case of David Morris. "We cannot admit anything openly because the Jewish faith is based on the theory that King David is Messiah and when he returns to earth the Kingdom of God will prevail. This means resurrection of the dead and other things, such as eternal justice, immortality and the like. I don't think the world, mankind, or even we Israelis are ripe for it yet. But if the boy is not Messiah, he cannot be King David—provided one believes in reincarnation."

At this time we can only speculate about the significance of the alleged reincarnation of King David in the person of young David Morris. It may be that the boy has been chosen as some very special clay for the divine molder and shaper of souls. Alan Leo, writing in his *Esoteric Astrology*, states that when the time for birth comes, a body is selected of a special type which is suitable for the soul's acquisition of the experience which is needed at that special time.

"It is not that the body by long-continued effort is wrought into the likeness of the soul," Leo writes, "but that the type of body is arranged beforehand to suit and express the type of Personality which requires manifestation during this earth-life. In short, the body is made to fit the personality just as a suit of clothes is made to fit the body.... The body is a living mask which hides, and yet at the same time expresses, the man who wears it."

Author Berry Benson once phrased the dogma of reincarnation in the analogy of a small boy who enters school and is placed by his teacher in the lowest class and charged with learning these lessons: Thou shalt not kill. Thou shalt do no hurt to any living thing. Thou shalt not steal.

So the little boy grew into a man. He did not kill, but he

became cruel and he stole. At the end of the day "when his beard was gray; when the night had come," the teacher noted that although the student had not killed, he had failed to learn his other lessons. "Come back again tomorrow," the teacher told him.

When the new day dawned, the pupil returned to school and was placed in a higher class because he had accomplished one lesson. Then the teacher gave him these lessons to learn: Thou shalt do not hurt to any living thing. Thou shalt not cheat. Thou shalt not steal. Again the boy grew into a man. He was careful to do no hurt to any living thing, and he tried not to be cruel. But he stole from his neighbors and he cheated to accomplish his own ends. At the end of the day, "when his beard was gray; when the night had come," the teacher recognized the fact that the student had learned to be merciful, but he had failed to accomplish the other lessons. Once again, the student was told to return on the morrow.

So it may be with man. Jesus Christ admonished man to be perfect even as God is perfect. Such perfection cannot be achieved in a single lifetime. It would seem more just to allow a man to return again and again, until all the "lessons" have been learned, before his soul stands to judgment and is examined as to whether it is worthy of attaining eternal life in the God Consciousness or should be shut away from God's grace.

"Even the best men are not, when they die, in such a state of intellectual and moral perfection as would fit them to enter heaven immediately," commented John M. Ellis McTaggart in *Some Dogmas of Religion*. McTaggart speculates that the man who dies after acquiring knowledge might enter his new life deprived of that particular bit of knowledge, " ... but not deprived of the increased strength and delicacy of mind which he gained in acquiring the knowledge ... So a man may carry over into his next life the disposition and tendencies which he has gained by the moral contests of this life, and the value of those experiences will not have been destroyed by the death which has destroyed the memory of them."

The doctrine of reincarnation obviously calls for a new way of regarding death. McTaggart says that death acquires a " ... new and deeper significance when we regard it no longer as a single and unexplained break in an unending life, but as part of the continually recurring rhythm of progress— as inevitable, as natural, and as benevolent as sleep. We have only left youth behind us, as at noon we have left the sunrise. They will both come back to us, and they do not grow old."

In *Reincarnation: A Study of the Human Soul*, Dr. Jerome Anderson draws an analogy between the universal repetition of rebirth with vegetable life's cyclic laws of regeneration, and he terms this process a "deep and basic law." The blossom perishes as completely as if it had never existed. But Dr. Anderson observes that the root rhizome, or bulb, holds in "subjective embrace" the most minute details of that flower. When the subjective cycle, the basic law, is fulfilled, the "subjective entity thrills, expands, clothes itself again with its vestment of cells and reproduces the plant in all its former perfection and beauty." Thus do the flowers reincarnate and express the same "elemental soul" of the plant.

Dr. Anderson also takes an example from the process of metamorphosis in insects, in which the subjective force is transferred from one organism to another. If nature has provided for the subjective cycles of flowers by the evolution of the bulb, Dr. Anderson remarks, "how much more reasonable it is that the intense individualization in man should also be conserved by subjective periods in his life-history. That the conditions limiting his consciousness in each state are different is no argument against these existing. The consciousness of a butterfly differs vastly from that of a caterpillar...." In Dr. Anderson's opinion " ... it logically follows ... that the individualization, carried to so marked an extent as it is in man, should be provided with subjective periods in which to assimilate and make its own the experiences of the last physical life."

If reincarnation is a part of reality, ask both the skeptical and the seekers, why do we not remember our past lives?

Sir Arthur Conan Doyle spoke about the question and expressed his opinion that such remembrance would " ... enormously complicate our present life and that such existences may well form a cycle which is all clear to us when we come to the end of it, when perhaps we may see a whole rosary of lives threaded upon one personality."

At the same time, vague recognitions and memories may influence the subconscious and cause one to behave in a manner which neither he nor his friends and family can explain. In some cases, being made aware of a past condition in what appears to have been a previous life can accomplish marvelous therapy on conditions that have become traumatic.

Dr. Louis Bluth of Sun City, California, told me of a case in which a young mother felt an overwhelming urge to murder her own children. Dr. Bluth placed the woman in light trance and learned that in her most recent incarnation, prior to her present state of existence, she had been a slave on a Southern plantation and had been forced to produce child after child for the slave market, as if she were a brood mare. The resentment the woman had felt at such degradation had survived as a subconscious memory.

Once the woman had heard the tape recording made of her session, she seemed relieved of a terrible burden of guilt and responded rapidly to therapy.

I met with the woman and found her to be an attractive young mother, who seemed to beam with the radiance of inner peace. "I don't know what I would have done without that session when I found out about my past life," she told me. "It gave me a new understanding of my problem and a new means of dealing with that terrible compulsion. To think that I might have killed my children!"

"No," her husband interjected, "I'm afraid we would have had you in an institution where you would not have been able to harm anyone."

It was hard to believe that the lovely, smiling young woman standing before me had once been branded a potential murderess, a mother so untrustworthy that her husband could not leave her alone with their own children.

What a new perspective such studies in hypnotic regression might give psychology in the diagnosis and treatment of mental problems! How daring it is in the Western world to consider that the source of the phobia or compulsion may not be found in the present life, but that its origin might be discovered by regressing the patient back to another existence.

It may be some time before such a suggestion receives a very enthusiastic reception among the majority of psychiatrists and psychotherapists, but Dr. Denys Kelsey, a British psychiatrist, believes that reincarnation is a fact and that a sick mind may be reborn in successive births. Because of his acceptance of the cycle of reincarnation, Dr. Kelsey endeavors to show his patients how they might begin anew at any given moment.

"The work I've done in the last seven years," Dr. Kelsey told Douglas Neale of United Press International, "has convinced me that it is occasionally possible for a subject to recall experiences which were felt ... centuries before their present incarnation."

Belief in the doctrine of rebirth may have come a bit easier to Dr. Kelsey than it does for the average psychiatrist, for he is married to Joan Grant, an authoress who claims that she is 25,000 years old and gives evidence of remembering thirty previous lives. Joan Grant has written seven historical novels without doing a bit of research, yet none of the material in her books has ever been successfully challenged by scholars. In fact, a good deal of the material which was considered new and controversial at the time of publication has since been validated by archaeologists and historians. Always, when queried how she could have acquired such knowledge, Joan Grant attributes her accuracy to memories of her past lives.

Winged Pharoah, the novel which Joan Grant wrote in 1937, described her life as a woman pharoah in the first dynasty of Egypt, 4,000 years ago. Commenting on the almost biblical style in which the book is written, she told journalist Neale that the words just came out in that manner.

"I believe that technically it's called five foot iambic. I never did any research at all. I knew nothing of Egypt; yet experts on Egyptology have been unable to fault the book. You know, when it was published critics said that I couldn't possibly have made it all up, that I must have experienced it all to write it in such detail. And none of the reviewers knew me personally."

Joan Grant's remarkable memories, if memories they be, make her the exception, rather than the rule, when it comes to being able to recall spontaneously one's past lives.

When an English clergyman spoke against reincarnation and concluded by stating that such alleged pre-existences could have no moral meaning simply because man was unable to remember anything about them, Dr. Leslie Weatherhead, minister of London's City Temple, answered, "So if some drug were given to [the clergyman] blotting out the memory of his youth, any indiscretions of that youth could have 'no present moral meaning'! He forgets that they would just as effectively have made him and molded him to be what he is, as if he remembered them. A judge is not often ready to excuse a prisoner of all moral responsibility if he asserts that he can't remember anything about it now!"

Dr. Weatherhead reminds the cleric that no one can consciously remember his earliest years, yet any psychologist will stress the importance of such a period in our development and will convince us of the effect this period had on us.

"The childhood incidents happened," Dr. Weatherhead says, "not to another, but to us, and, though now forgotten, determined many of our present reactions to life. The very pattern of adult life is a form of stored memory. We do not need to remember mental impressions to be influenced by them."

Creative people often seem to be given glimpses of their past lives. The old records, journals and biographies of artists, poets and writers are filled with such allusions, but we need not dip back into dusty tomes to find such an illustration. Broadway lyricist Allan J. Lerner stated (*Atlantic Monthly*, November, 1965) that the first act ending of his

Brigadoon, which features an outdoor wedding ceremony in the Scotland of the seventeenth century, seemed to have sprung spontaneously from his mind. Several years later, when Lerner was in London, he came into possession of a book entitled *Everyday Life in Old Scotland* and found "his" marriage ceremony word for word.

Lerner's later musical success, *On a Clear Day You Can See Forever*, tells the story of a Brooklyn model who is regressed to an earlier life in eighteenth century England. In explaining his motivation for writing a musical play about such a controversial subject as rebirth, Lerner said, " ... I had become increasingly outraged at all the pat explanations psychoanalysis was throwing up to explain human behavior. I was becoming more and more disgusted by the morality of psychoanalysis—that we are living in a world where there is no more character and where everything is behavior; that there is no more good, it is all adjustment; that there is no more evil, it is all maladjustment. Psychoanalysis has turned into a totally unsatisfactory religion which gives no life hereafter, and no divine morality to live by. And so I began to think ... I would find a way of saying I don't think that we are all that explainable; that much of us is still unknown; that there are vast worlds within us. ..."

Gustave Geley was a tireless explorer of those "vast worlds." Geley believed that the visible, external body, which is subject to birth and death, limited in its powers, ephemeral in its duration, is not the "real being." The real stuff of personality, or self, " ... is the divine spark on the way to realize its divinity, of unlimited potentialities, creative and eternal."

Geley saw the fact that the vast majority have no memory of their past lives as " ... as great a blessing as ignorance of the future. ... If the commonplace man had but a flash of this knowledge, he would be dumfounded by it. His present errors and anxieties are as much as he can bear. ... Remembrance of the past could but impede present effort. ..."

In Book V of his *Ethics*, Spinoza reflected that even though it may not always be possible for man to remember

previous lives, all men have an inner awareness that they are
eternal. Man is able to perceive that his mind is eternal " ...
in so far as it involves the body's essence under the category
of eternity, and that this, its existence, cannot be defined by
time or interpreted by duration."

Lessing wondered why reincarnation should be so laugh-
able to his contemporaries merely because it is the oldest of
man's hypotheses. In Lessing's view, man's basic understanding hit upon reincarnation as the logical philosophy long
before "the sophistries of the schools" had dissipated and
debilitated it. "Why should I not come back as often as I am
capable of acquiring fresh knowledge, fresh alertness?" Lessing asked in his *The Divine Education of the Human Race.*
"Do I bring away so much from once that there is nothing to
repay the trouble of coming back? Is this a reason against it?
Or, because I forget that I have been here already? Happy it
is for me that I do forget. The recollection of my former
condition would permit me to make only a bad use of the
present."

Pythagoras (582 to 500 B.C.) is reported to have been the
first of the Greeks to teach the doctrine that the soul, passing
through the "circle of necessity," was born at various times to
various living bodies. Plato alludes to reincarnation in many
of his essays and he seems to be speaking of the ethics of
Karma in Book X of *Laws* when he says: "Know that if you
become worse you will go to the worse souls, or if better to
the better, and in every succession of life and death you will
do and suffer what like may fitly suffer at the hands of like."

Cicero's *Treatise on Glory* concedes that " ... the counsels
of the Divine Mind had some glimpses of truth when they
said that men are born in order to suffer the penalty for
some sins committed in a former life."

The chief theological work of the Hindus, the *Upanishads*,
expresses the doctrine of rebirth in the poetic imagery of a
goldsmith who takes a raw piece of gold and shapes it into
another, more beautiful form. "So, verily, the Self, having
cast off this body and having put away ignorance, makes
another new and more beautiful form."

In his *Exhortations to the Pagans,* the Christian writer St. Clement of Alexandria does more than echo St. Augustine's plaintive query of whether or not man had an existence prior to the one before he entered his mother's womb. "We were in being long before the foundation of the world," St. Clement believed. "We existed in the eye of God, for it is our destiny to live in Him. We are the reasonable creatures of the Divine Word; therefore we have existed from the beginning, for in the beginning was the Word. . . . Not for the first time does He show pity on us in our wanderings; He pitied us from the very beginning."

Annie Besant observed that life gains security and dignity when it can be seen with a long vista. Death becomes but a mere incident in life, a change of scene, a brief journey. "The links of the present are found to be a part of a golden chain that stretches backwards, and the future can be faced with a glad security in the thought that these links will endure through days to come and form part of that unbroken chain," she writes in *The Ancient Wisdom.*

"With reincarnation man is a dignified, immortal being, evolving towards a divinely glorious end; without it, he is a tossing straw on the stream of chance circumstances, irresponsible for his character, for his actions, for his destiny."

CHAPTER IV

THE REBIRTH OF ABIGAIL DAWS

"You have forgotten your childhood, though you have the same physical brain now. In another life, you had a different brain. ... It is only the Spirit which passes from life to life, with its three great qualities of Will, Cognition, and Activity. The whole of the rest of you is new with each birth, and before the Heavenly Life is over, all the experience which has been changed into character is handed on to the Spirit that dies not ... If, then, you are to remember, you must reach the memory of the Spirit."—Annie Besant, from a lecture on reincarnation.

Shortly after Bill Williams, his son Jack, and George Field had returned from their expedition to Jefferson, North Carolina, a young woman named Mary Tobbin came to the Williams' home and asked if the hypnotist could help clear up a mild skin rash on her arm. Bill is intensely interested in the medical application of hypnosis, especially in the diagnostic aspects. Of course, he never prescribes for any illness and he does not pretend for one moment to accomplish miracle healings, but the minor complaints which fall into the area of the psychosomatic can often be cleared up through the application of hypnotic power of suggestion.

Mary Tobbin proved to be an excellent hypnotic subject. She went into light trance quickly and easily. After Bill had planted the suggestion that her skin rash would disappear, he brought Mary back to full consciousness and obtained her

71

consent to place her into a deep trance state so that he might attempt to regress her. Mary readily granted her permission, and the following remarkable transcription is a result of that initial session.

Oh, oh, I see some rats! Yeah, all sorts of rats!

Where are they?

They're on a ship.

Are you on the ship?

Yeah, I'm on a ship.

What's your name?

Abigail. Abigail Daws.

And where is this ship going?

It's suppose' to go to America.

Oh, what year is this?

1692.

Where does this ship come from?

England.

How old are you?

I'm fourteen.

I see. Who is with you on this ship? Your mother and your father?

No, I'm by myself.

How come you're all alone?

I'm a servant.

Whose servant?

I don't know.

You don't know their name?

No.

How do you know who to work for if you don't know them?

I'm going to find out.

Oh, I see. They're not with you. Well, were you sold to someone in America? [Abigail appears to have been an indentured servant.]

Yeah, I lost my money and they put me in jail.

I'm going to count to three and we'll go back two months when you were still in England. One, two, three! Now what are you doing, Abigail?

I'm in jail.

Why?

I stold some bread.

Do you have a mother and father?

No, they're dead.

How long have they been dead?

About five years.

And how old are you?

I'm (slight pause) *fourteen.*

So you stole some bread and they put you in jail. How long are they going to keep you there?

I don't know, maybe forever.

Well, I'll count to three, and we'll take you to the day that they're going to let you out of there. One, two, three! Now what's going on?

They tell me I'm going away, that I'm going to America. I don't want to go. I don't want to go there!

Who's telling you all this?

A man, a big man. I don't know who he is. He's nasty. He's a big man. He's got black hair and a black beard, and he smells dirty. Ugh, he smells awful!

We'll count to three and you will be on the other side of the water; you will be in America. One, two, three. Now what do you see?

Getting off the ship. It's coming into Virginia.

Virginia, what port in Virginia?

I don't know! I never heard of it.

Are there many people there?

(Abigail begins to cough violently.)

What's the matter? I'll count to three and your cough will stop. One, two, three. What was the matter?

I have a bad cough.

Where did you get that, on the ship?

No, I had it before.

How long have you had it?

About a month, I guess.

Does it get worse?

Yeah, I don't feel very well.

Does it make you spit up blood?

Yes, sometimes.

You say the ship is just coming into town? Okay, it will be one week later so you can be settled. One, two, three. Now what do you see?

I'm working in the kitchen.

Whose kitchen?

The Jacksons.

What town is it in Virginia?

Richmond.

How did you get to Richmond from the boat?

In a cart.

How long did that take?

About a day.

Do you remember the town where the boats stop?

Don't remember.

Did you hear it at all?

No. I was sick.

How do you feel now?

Not very well. They don't make me work very hard, those people.

They're pretty good to you?

Yes.

What kind of a place do they have?

A big place, real nice. They have lots of land. (Another fit of coughing)

We'll count to three and the coughing will stop. One, two, three. What do they raise on this farm?

Oh, some vegetables and some chickens, and they have some cotton.

Do they have a lot of help?

Yes, they have a lot of help.

Do they have slaves or what?

They have the nigras, they're called. [Black slaves were first brought to Virginia—and the Colonies—in 1619. After 1690, large numbers of slaves were brought to the plantations to fill the demand for cheap labor.]

But you're white help?

Yeah.

You just work in the kitchen?

Yeah.

What do you do—cook, wash dishes, or what?

I bake bread.

Oh, I see. Who does the cooking?

The black mammy.

Do you get good food?

Yes, pretty good.

Do you get lots of it?

No, there's too many of us.

What do you have to eat?

Onions, carrots, a lot of beans.

What do you have for meat?

Salt pork. Ech! I hate that!

How do you make this bread?

Well, you take some flour, the flour they grind down ... and you knead it.... Then you let it set: you let it set overnight. Then you knead it ... and ... put it into little things.

How many loaves do you have to make a day?

Oh, maybe fourteen or maybe thirteen, lots and lots of them. Then you put it into the oven.

What do you have for an oven?

It's a great big thing.

What is it made of?

Oh, bricks, lots of bricks.

How do you heat it?

With wood.

We'll count to three, and it will be five years later, and you will tell me what's going on. One, two, three. Now what do you see?

Nothing. [The death experience has taken place.]

What are you doing?

Floating.

All right, I'll count to three again, and we'll go back to your last day as Abigail. One, two, three. Now what do you see?

(Violent spasms of coughing)

Abigail, you don't have to cough. I'll count to three and your coughing will stop. One, two, three. All right, you don't have to cough; you can tell us what 's going on.

I'm sick.

Where are you?

I'm in a house.

Whose house?

The work house.

Where are the Jacksons?

They're gone away. They're always gone away.

How old are you now?

I must be about seventeen. Yeah, I'm seventeen.

How long have you been here?

It must be three years.

Do you like it here?

Yes, it's nice and peaceful here, and the sun shines.

Do you like it better than England?

Yes.

So you're glad you came over?

Yes, I'm glad I came over here.

How do you feel? How has this cough of yours been?

Awful! It gets worse.

Do you still spit up blood now and then?

Oh, yes, all the time. Yes.

They don't do anything for it? There's nothing you can do?

No.

We'll go along and you can tell us what happens now. One, two, three. Tell me what's happening now.

I'm awful sick. I keep coughing and coughing, and I keep spitting up blood. I'm dying, and people tell me I'm dying.

Are you glad you're dying?

No, I don't want to die! I don't want to die! (Becoming hysterical) *No, I'm too young to die! I don't want to die, no! I can't die! I'm too young! I don't want to die! I'm too young to die!*

I'll count to three and it will be all over with. One, two, three. Now what do you see?

Nothing. [The tone of the voice is now relaxed, almost to
the point of total indifference.]

Where are you?

Floating.

Can you see your body there?

Yep.

What's happened to it?

Nothing. It's lying there.

Where?

On the bed.

Is anybody attending to it?

Yes. The black mammy.

What's she doing?

She's cleaning me up, Oh, yeah.

Oh, now what's she doing?

She's lifting me into a pretty dress.

She's quite nice to you.

Yes, she is; she's good. Yes.

Now what's going on?

People are walking by.

Do they have you in a box or anything?

Yeah.

What kind of a box?

A pine one.

Are the Jacksons there?

No.

Who is coming by?

All the nigras.

Are they all good friends of yours?

Yeah, I'm friendly.

Now what's happening?

Nothing.

Do they have a preacher or anyone for you?

Yeah.

What's he have to say?

He just says I'm nice. Yeah, I was a good girl.

Is that all he says?

Yeah.

What do they say at the grave?
They just say from ashes to ashes, from dust to dust. Then they throw me in the grave. They cover me over.
What are you doing, just floating and watching all this?
Yeah.
It doesn't bother you to watch?
Naw.
It doesn't hurt a bit, does it?
Naw.
Are you glad now that you died?
Yes!
It's a lot better, isn't it?
Yeah, I like it! I like to float!
You're just floating?
Yep.
I'm going to count to three, and you will wake up in the present time. You're going to feel very relaxed and very, very rested. Better than you have in a long, long time. One, you're starting to wake up. Two, your eyes are beginning to open now. Three, you're wide awake and feeling fine.

In his *The Destiny of Man*, J. G. Fichte argued that since man is not a product of the world of sense, his existence can never be attained in that world. Man's ultimate destination, it would seem, lies beyond time and space and all things connected with the world of sense. Pierre Leroux points out that if we learn to regard the world as a series of successive lives, we may be able to perceive, at least partially, how God, for whom neither time nor space exists, can permit suffering as being a necessary phase men must pass in order to reach a state of true happiness which we cannot conceive from our mortal viewpoint.

"A lifetime may be needed merely to gain the virtues which annul the errors of man's preceding life," said the novelist Honoré de Balzac. "The virtues we acquire, which develop slowly within us, are the invisible links which bind each one of our existences to the others—existences which the spirit alone remembers. . . ."

In another session of hypnotic regression, Mary Tobbin recalled a life in which she was born a boy in the United States about 1840. She describes in great detail her life as a farm boy who lives with an abandoned mother and a younger sister. When he is in his early teens, the boy leaves home and goes in search of the father who deserted them. Although he spends a good deal of time wandering about the countryside, he never finds his father.

When the Civil War breaks out, the young man, who has become something of a misanthrope, refuses to bear arms, but he does serve as a drummer for the Union forces. After the war he completely withdraws from the society of men and becomes a hermit. He lives alone in the woods for the rest of his long life, surrounded by Jolly, his pet bear, a raccoon that sleeps on his bed at night, and other animal friends. It should be noted that the hermit's speech patterns are markedly different from those of either Mary Tobbin or Abigail Daws.

This tape is most remarkable as it records the encroaching old age of the hermit and his death scene. The voice of the narrator becomes weary and enfeebled. Associations become slow and confused.

At one point on the tape, when Williams asks the hermit if he would like to live another eighty years, the old man replies, "Oh, I couldn't stand it!"

An acceptance of death is clearly seen as the hermit observes that "it's about that time. I'm gettin' ready to go."

A friend, who had died several years before the hermit's own reported demise, circa 1910, stops by for a visit in his ethereal form. This is one of the many cases which Williams has on tape in which a deathbed visitation is reported by the dying subject.

When the hermit passes on, he, too, reports his eesential self floating above the body. He is resentful of two trappers who stop by the cabin and bury him. "I don't know those men, and I don't like them!" he complains.

He watches the men putting his body in a crude coffin and

covering it with dirt. He reports this without emotion, because, "it isn't me in there."

At this point, Bill asked the entity to "float" on for another ten years. "Who are you now?" the hypnotist asked the disembodied soul.

The entity gives the name which it possessed as the hermit, then pauses as if uncertain. "I think that's who I am."

Another ten years and the entity must struggle to remember the hermit's name. At Bill's next count the entity states that it has no name.

Throughout his research, Williams has found an average of approximately eighty years between lives. He is by no means dogmatic about this finding, and, obviously, this case was to prove an exception, because, according to the hermit, he died in 1910, and the young woman sitting before Williams had been born in 1943. Bill was determined to lead the entity up to the birth experience in its present incarnation.

Are you still floating?

Yeah, I'm just floating.

You're going to float on a little more, a little more, nearer today now. What do you see?

I don't know. I don't know, just things.

What things?

Just things. I don't know. People. There's a field near a beach. There's lots of people.

What's your name?

I don't know. I don't have a name.

Are you still floating?

No, I'm there! I'm watching!

What are the people doing?

I don't know! (Becoming excited) *I don't know what they're doing, but they're awful. They're hurting him! It's awful! They're awful,* (beginning to cry) *they're hurting him!*

We'll go on to three years later. One, two, three! Now what do you see?

I see a house.

Where?

I don't know. It's just a little house. It's cute.

What's your name?

Mar-r-y. (Drawing out the name in little girl fashion)

How old are you?

Two!

We're going back to your first day as Mary. You can tell me all about that. One, two, three. Now what do you see?

Black.

I see. What are you doing?

Nothing.

Where are you?

I don't know.

All you see is black?

Yep.

In just a few minutes now you will have to see something. One, two, three. Now what do you see?

White.

Where are you?

I don't know. Oh, look at the people! Oh!

What are they doing?

I don't know. Oh, a lady there!

What's she doing?

I don't know!

What's she got on?

White.

What do you have on?

Nothing.

How big are you?

I'm little. Yeah, real little! Awful little!

What's your name?

Mar-r-y.

How old are you?

I'm about two minutes old!

Do you remember being born?

Nope. All those people are happy. Ha-ha! Ha-ha! (Begins to laugh wildly)

I'll count to three now, and it will be the next day. One, two, three. It's the next day. What do you have on today?

A pink nightie.

Do you like that? Is it comfortable?

Yeah, I like it. (Then, changing her mind) *My hands are tied in, though; I don't like that. I don't like my hands tied. It's awful.*

I'm going to count to three, and it will be six months later. One, two, three. Now what do you see?

I'm with my daddy. I've never seen him before. He's my daddy, though. [Mary Tobbin's father had been in military service at the time of her birth and was unable to see his child until she was six months old.]

What are you doing?

I'm on my daddy's lap, and they're taking pictures of me.

Is that fun?

No, I don't like that. I cry.

What do you have on? Are you all dressed up for the pictures?

I've got a pretty white dress on. Yeah, it's got green, white and red things on it. It has white and green things down like this, and great big green buttons, and white and green things around it like this. It's cute. I like it. My hair is curly.

CHAPTER V

THE MAN WHO LOVED THE MOUNTAINS

The case of Charles Riley offers no real clues toward a firm substantiation of the entity's professed memories of a life in the Rocky Mountain region of Montana, but the transcript is fascinating in its characterization of a latter-day "mountain man," in the details of the death experience and in the progression to the present incarnation. The young man who related this alleged former life while hypnotically regressed had no conscious memory of his existence as Morton Smith. Even while placed in a light trance, Charles Riley denied ever having heard of the mountain man or of knowing anyone by that name.

As has been stated before in previous chapters, the absence of memory of any previous state does not constitute a conclusive argument against one's having lived through a previous life. Professor William Knight once remarked that forgetfulness of the past may be one of the conditions of an entrance upon a new stage of existence. "The body, which is the organ of self-perception, may be quite as much a hindrance as a help of remembrance," stated Professor Knight. "In that case, casual gleams of memory, giving us sudden abrupt and momentary revelations of the past, are precisely the phenomena we would expect to meet with. If the soul has pre-existed, what we would *a priori* anticipate are only some faint traces of recollection surviving in the crypts of memory."

Bill Williams is convinced that hypnosis is man's greatest

aid in prying loose the rusted recollections which might lie in such "crypts of memory." Here are selections from the regression of Charles Riley-Morton Smith.

You say that your name is Morton Smith. How old are you?

About twenty.

And you live in Montana. Do you know any of the names of the towns near where you live?

I don't remember what the name of the town is. Fact is, I haven't been there for a long time.

How big a town is it?

There's not very many people, maybe about a couple of hundred.

Are you married?

No.

Why not?

I want to stay up here in the mountains.

A woman would be just a problem?

Yeah.

I'm going to count to three and it will be five years later. One, two, three. Now what do you see, Morton?

I'm helping the old man. [An old trapper with whom Morton lived]

What's the matter?

He's in bed. He's got a bad leg.

What happened to his leg?

He fell down and got a bad cut.

What are you doing about it?

Putting some rags on it.

How is it coming along?

Well, it's healing; it's better than yesterday.

How's the hunting and trapping?

Good.

Making a lot of money?

Enough to get by on.

How old are you now?

I would say around twenty-five, somewhere around there.

Still haven't got married?

No!

Aren't there any good-looking girls in town when you do get there?

Well, last year there was one, but she never paid any attention to me.

You probably didn't have money enough. That's the way these women are. I'm going to count to three, and you will be five years older. One, two, three. Now what are you doing?

Hunting.

Is the old man still there?

No, he died.

When did he die?

A couple years ago, I guess.

What was the matter with him?

He got shot.

How did that happen?

He fell down.

Did he shoot himself with his own rifle?

Yes.

Did he die right away?

Shot himself in the head.

Were you there?

No. A man down from the valley found him.

Did you have a big funeral for him?

No.

What did you do?

Townspeople buried him. I knew about it; I just didn't want to go down.

Why not?

Too many people around. Some of them are all dressed up and everything. I got all homemade clothes on.

What are your clothes made of?

Deer hide.

How old are you now?

Probably about twenty-nine.

What year is this?

1870, I guess.

I'm going to count to three, and it will be five years later. One, two, three. Now what are you doing?

Going up the mountains.

Hunting?

No, walking with my wife.

Wife! What happened?

Well, I went into the valley and met this woman and married her.

How long have you been married?

Three hours.

Oh, I see. You're going on your honeymoon. Where are you going, up to your cabin?

Yeah.

Well, let's go on a little bit farther until we get up to your cabin and see what happens. Now what are you doing?

Getting supper.

You have to do the cooking?

I don't have to.

Does your wife cook?

Don't know.

What's she doing, then?

Sitting there.

And you're getting supper for her? What's she have to say?

She just didn't think the carrots were very good.

What are you fixing for supper?

Deer meat. Carrots and things.

How does she like that?

I don't know how she likes it, but I like it.

Let's go on in time a little bit until you're through eating supper. Tell me what she says about it.

She thinks it's okay, for a man's cooking.

What's her name?

Hannah.

Let's go on a couple more hours. What's she doing?

She's going to go to bed out in the front room.

How come she isn't sleeping with you?

She's mad at me.

Why?

I don't know; I must have said something.

That's quite a wedding night isn't it? She's in the front room and you're there. What's she sleeping on?

Rug.

And you got the bed, right?

Yeah!

Now I'm going to count to three, and it will be five years later. One, two, three. Now what are you doing?

Feeding the baby.

How many babies do you have?

Just one.

Why do you have to feed it? Doesn't Hannah do that?

She's gone down to the village.

What for, shopping?

Get some flour.

How far is it to the village?

A mile an' a half, two miles maybe.

How do you get along with her? Do you still fight?

Not very often.

Does she still sleep on the rug?

No.

So you got that all patched up! Who does the cooking?

She does.

How old is your baby?

Oh, about three months.

A boy or a girl?

Boy.

What's his name?

Tommy.

Are you still hunting and trapping?

Oh, yeah.

I'm going to count to three and it will be five years later. One, two, three. Now what are you doing?

I just got back from outside.

What have you been doing?

Bringing in some firewood.

Is it wintertime?

Yes.

How cold does it get there?
Oh, up where we are, about 30 below.
How's the wife?
She's getting fat!
Any more kids?
Yeah.
How many do you have now?
Two.
Both boys?
Yeah.
What's the other boy's name?
Danny.
You say that Hannah is getting fat?
Yeah.
You're probably feeding her too much.
She feeds herself.
What are you having for dinner today?
Squirrels.
What else?
She got some onions.
Do you like onions?
No!
She does?
Yeah. That's why she gets fat!
Onions aren't fattening.
Well, something's doing it!
I'm going to count to three again, and it will be five years later. One, two, three. Now what are you doing?
Settin' in the house.
No trapping or hunting today?
It's raining out.
How old are you now?
I must be about thirty-five, forty maybe. Getting old.
How's the trapping going?
Not too good now. Can't move around too good.
Why, what happened?
I broke my leg.
How did you do that?

I fell out of a tree.
What the heck were you doing up a tree?
Going after a 'coon.
How's Hannah?
She's not too bad.
Is she still getting fat?
If she gets any fatter, I don't know what I'll do.
Why, what's the matter?
Just about can't move around now.
It must make the bed kind of crowded, doesn't it?
I sleep on the rug!
Don't you ever crawl in bed?
No!
Why?
No room!
It must get kind of cold on the rug in the wintertime, doesn't it?
Dog sleeps with me.
You like that better than the wife?
Dog doesn't talk as much.
Kind of sorry you brought Hannah home?
Not really.
Just wish she would lose some weight?
Yes!
I'm going to count to three and it will be five years later. One, two, three. Now what are you doing?
Going down the mountains.
How's your leg?
Not very good.
It still bothers?
Guess so.
Do you still do some hunting?
Not any more.
What do you do for a living now?
I just stay in the house.
How do you live?
The boys do it all. Tommy must be somewhere around

*seventeen, Danny about twelve, somewhere in there. I don't
know for sure.*

How's the wife?

She died.

What happened to her?

Too fat, I guess.

How long ago did she die?

About six months.

Who does the cooking now?

Tommy.

He does the cooking and the hunting and you just sit.
What do you do when you just sit, do you read?

Never learned to read.

Do you write?

No.

Do you write your own name?

No.

What do you do if you have to sign something?

Just put an x on it.

How about the boys, do they go to school?

No.

It must kind of lonesome there if you can't read.

I whittle.

What do you whittle?

Oh, statues.

Are you good at it?

Not very.

How old are you now?

Pretty close to fifty now.

I'm going to count to three and it will be five years later.
One, two, three. How what are you doing?

Still settin' in the chair.

The boys still around?

Only one of them, Tommy.

What happened to the other one?

*He went down the mountain one day and never came
back.*

Did he get married or something?

I don't know. I never heard from him.

Just you and Tommy. Does he still do the hunting and the trapping and so on?

Oh, yeah.

I'm going to count to three and it will be five years later. One, two, three. Now what are you doing?

Walking around on crutches.

How come on crutches? Your leg isn't getting any better?

It's been bad for a long time.

Tommy still around?

Oh, yeah.

Have you ever heard from Danny?

No, never heard from him.

Tom get married yet?

No.

How old is he now?

He must be about twenty-six, seven.

He's getting big enough to get a wife, isn't he?

He's got a girl friend.

Now I'm going to count to three and it will be five years later. One, two, three. Now what do you see?

I'm in bed.

Is your leg getting worse?

Can't even walk now.

Tom still around?

Oh, yeah.

Did he ever get married?

Oh, yeah.

Is his wife living there with you?

No. She won't live here.

Where does she live?

Down in the village.

Does Tom have a house there, too?

Yeah.

How does he keep both of them going?

He stays with me all week and goes home once in a while.

Does he still go hunting?

Hunts and sells furs.

How long has he been married?
Oh, a year and a half, two years maybe.
You don't feel very good now?
No.
How long have you been in bed?
Couple months.
Is it the leg?
'Way up through! It hurts like the devil!
I'm going to count to three and it will be five years later.
One, two, three. Now what are you doing?
Just settin' up there.
Where? What do you see?
Just a lot of things floating around. [The death experience
has occurred.]
Where's Tom?
I don't know.
You can see him if you look. [Morton is now outside the
confines of time and space.]
He's working in a saloon.
Are you still alive?
Don't think so.
But you can see Tom if you want to?
Guess I can.
Do you watch him much?
No.
Do you ever watch him to see what he's doing?
Once in a while I look.
Do you ever try to speak to him?
No.
Are you comfortable?
Yes.
Did you ever find Danny?
No.
Do you think you can see him where you are now?
I don't know.
Let's try.
There's a lot of people down there.
Where are you?

I don't know where I am, but it's not too bad up here.
It's comfortable?
Yeah.
What do you do?
Just set, and I'll walk around.
Do you ever see anyone you know?
Yeah, once in a while.
The old man who used to live with you?
Oh, yeah, I see him.
How about your father?
No, never seen him up there.
You do see people once in a while?
Yeah, once in a while.
I'm going to count to three again and we'll go back to your last day. One, two, three. Now what are you doing?
My leg hurts. It's awful sore.
How old are you now?
I must be about seventy-nine, eighty, I guess.
Where's Tom?
He's by the bed.
Have you had anything to eat today?
No.
Why?
Don't want anything.
How long since you ate?
A day or so maybe.
But you feel pretty good except for your leg?
Yeah. It's big!
All swollen up?
Yeah!
Time drifts along. Tell us what happens now, what's going on?
My leg turned green. It's all green! It stinks!
Now what's happening?
Tom is trying to get me to drink something. There's a man standing over there.
What's he doing?
He's got a thing on my chest. It's cold!

What's it look like?
It's got two little pipes on it. He sticks it in his ears.
You never saw anything like that before?
Never! It scares me!
What's he have to say?
He just keeps looking at Tom and shaking his head.
I wonder why.
I don't know!
Let time go on a little farther now. What's happening?
I'm just settin' up there.
Up where?
I don't know.
Let's go back to the last thing you remember.
Tom, settin' on a chair by the bed.
What are you doing?
Just laying there.
How do you feel?
Terrible.
Two, three minutes go by. What's going on?
Tom is holding my hand.
How do you feel?
Not very good.
It's a little later. What's going on now?
Somebody's poking at me!
Why?
I don't know!
How do you feel?
I feel pretty good.
What's Tom doing?
Crying.
Why?
I don't know. He's just setting there crying!
Do you feel better now?
Yeah.
Who's poking you?
That doctor! I heard Tom call him Dr. Thomas. He's got his head under my ... no ... he's got an eye over my head.

He's got me lifted up a little bit. He's patting me on the chest.

Do you feel it?

No!

We'll let a few more minutes go by and you tell me what you see.

Somebody down there looks just like me.

But you're not there?

Can't be!

Is it your body lying on the bed?

It looks like me.

Where's Tom?

Crying like the devil.

Is the doctor still there? What's he doing?

Just settin' in the chair, shaking his head.

Let time go on a little farther. You keep watching that body and tell us what they do with it.

Somebody pulled the blankets up over my face.

Does that bother you?

No.

How do you feel now?

Comfortable and good.

Now what are they doing to you?

They picked it up. [His body has now become "it," as his detachment toward his fleshly environment continues to grow.]

Who?

Tom and that doctor.

Now what are they doing?

They're putting it out in the shack.

Is it winter?

Yeah.

What are they doing now?

They came back in the room.

Is your body still in the shed?

Yeah. [This was a common practice in the last century.

When the soil of winter became too hard to spade, burial had to wait until spring.]

You're watching it there, are you?

Yeah, I can see it there.

Let's go on to the next day. Tell me what they do with that body out in the shed.

It's still there.

Are they doing anything about it?

They didn't do a thing to me.

Where's Tom?

He's back.

What's he doing?

He's building some kind of box. A long thing, with boards across the end.

What do you suppose he's going to do with that?

I don't know.

We'll just watch him, and we'll see what he's doing as time goes on. Now what are they doing with the box?

They're ... they're picking me up. They're carrying me.

Carrying you from where?

From the shed.

Can you feel it or do you see it?

I can see it; I don't feel anything.

Where are you, above somewhere watching?

Yeah, settin' up there somewhere.

Now what are they doing?

They're putting it in the box.

Let's go on in time until they do something with the box. Now what's happening?

The box is setting outside.

Is it still winter?

Yeah.

Who's around there now?

Tom, his wife, that doctor, a man all dressed up in a suit. A preacher, I guess.

What are they doing?

Just looking at the box.

Is it open?

No. The preacher is saying something.

What's he saying?

He's just talking how good I use' to be: how kind I was to the boys and everything. Now they're going to put their heads down and just look at the box. Tom and the doctor pick it up. They're going up through the woods with it. The doctor fell down.

Did he get hurt?

No, he got back up. They're going to a cave. Tom is shoveling away the snow. They pick up the box again, and they're going down with it. They just set the box on the floor.

Let's go on. Do they leave the box there?

Yeah.

How about next spring? Move ahead in time. Do you still see the box in the cave?

They caved the cave in.

They left the box in the cave? They didn't bother to dig a grave or anything?

No.

How long have you been watching, just floating?

Oh, I don't know. Been quite a while, I guess.

What year do you think this is?

Well, I don't know. It must be close to the turn of the century, I guess.

Do you see what's going on in the world?

I don't look down there much anymore.

You're very comfortable?

Yeah.

We're going to move ahead in time again until you remember being someone. One, two, three. Now what do you see?

A little crib.

What's your name?

Charles Riley.

Do you remember Morton?

Morton who?

Morton Smith. The one who lived in Montana.

I don't know Morton Smith.

I'm going to count to three and you will come back to the present time. You're going to feel very, very good. One ... two ...

CHAPTER VI

THERE IS NO DEATH, ONLY CHANGE

"I perceive an Apotheosis of Death. There is no death, only change, and always change with a purpose, change to a greater end. Death is re-creation, renewal, the dropping of fetters, the casting aside of a vehicle which has ceased to suffice. Death is, in very truth, a birth into a fuller and larger life, or a dipping down into matter under the law of readjustment. Progress always, and progress toward Unity. We come ever nearer to each other and to the Real through death."—George S. Arundale, *Nirvana.*

The four cases presented in this chapter have been included to demonstrate the hypothesis that there is no death, only change. In *The World as Will and Idea*, Schopenhauer expressed the thought that what sleep is for the individual, death is for the will. It was his view that the will, or soul, is refreshed by the sleep of death. "Every new-born being comes fresh and blithe into the new existence," Schopenhauer writes. " . . . Its fresh existence is paid for by the old age and death of a worn-out existence which has perished, but which contained the indestructible seed out of which the new existence has arisen; they are *one* being. . . ."

Subject number one came to Bill Williams because he was having some difficulty adjusting to a new situation on his job. He proved to be a good subject, and Williams brought him back to full consciousness to obtain his permission to regress him.

" ... Deeper and deeper asleep ... you're going to go way back, way, way back, back a hundred years or more, do you understand? You are going to go back until you see something; then you will stop and tell us what you see. I am going to count to three and you will go farther and farther back. One ... going back. Two, farther back. Three, way back. What do you see now?"

The young man seemed to have landed in a void. He said he saw nothing. He seemed to be between lives.

Williams took him back farther. "One ... going back. Two, something is coming into view. Three ... what do you see now?"

The young man said he saw a white house. A farmhouse. He was a young farmer watching his two sons as they played in the yard.

Williams: I think if you would look around the house you would find a newspaper. Yes, there's one, isn't there? Now pick it up and look at the date on it and tell me what year and month are printed on it.

Subject: May 11th. ...

Williams: What year?

Subject: 1846.

Williams: Where do you live?

Subject: I'm not certain.

Williams: Well, that would be printed on the newspaper, too. Look for it.

Subject: I see Illinois something ... Illinois *Gazette*, or something like that.

The subject could not make out a city, but he did recall that his name was Samuel Owens and that he was a twenty-six-year-old farmer with two sons, John and Bill. He could not remember his wife's name. The hypnotist tried moving Samuel Owens ten years ahead in time. Then he returned the subject to the present for an interlude of rest before they resumed regression. When the subject was placed back into trance, Williams "set" the year at 1862.

Williams: What do you see now?

Samuel: Fighting!

Samuel Owens was a "regular soldier" fighting, strangely enough, on the side of the Confederacy.

Williams: I thought you were from the North . . . from Illinois.

Samuel: I was, but I went with the Confederates. I just liked their side better.

Williams: What's going on around you?

Samuel: There's bullets flying all around, and men are dropping.

Williams: Who's winning?

Samuel: Nobody . . . we're just holding our ground.

Williams: Where are you?

Samuel: I don't remember. . . .

Williams: Do you know any of the people around you?

Samuel: My friend Bill. He's another soldier.

The Confederate soldier went on to describe the technique by which he fired his muzzle-loading military musket. He checked his timepiece and saw that it was 2:30 P.M. He moaned when he realized that the fighting had been going on since 10:30 A.M. Samuel was certain the year was 1862 and the month was February, but he could not recall the day. Williams brought the soldier forward another year in time. Samuel was now certain that they were in Richmond, Virginia, and that they were in the midst of another pitched battle.

What regiment are you in?

Ninth of Northern Virginia, I think.

Have you been in many battles in the last couple years?

Yes.

All were around Richmond?

All around and all over.

Where else?

I went to Georgia.

Did you get up North at all?

We started to, but we had to turn around.

I will count to three and it will be six months later. One,

you are getting older; two, still older; three ... what do you see now?

Nothing.

What are you doing?

Nothing.

Do you see anything?

No.

Are you alive?

I don't think so.

I will now count to three and it will be your last day as Samuel. One, we're going back; two, still farther back; three ... what do you see now?

We're fighting.

Where?

I don't know, but we're coming up over a hill.

You don't know what state you're in or anything?

No.

Is it a big battle?

Yes, we have them on the run.

What's the date?

It is May '63.

What day or night?

May 5th, I think.

You have the Yankees running?

Yeah.

Now what are you doing?

I'm still coming up over the hill.

Let's get up over there and see what happens.

We start to get them on the run. And then I heard shots and that was all there was.

What do you mean?

I heard shots and I just fell.

Did you feel anything?

No.

Let's go back to when you hear these shots and tell me what you feel. Are you hit now? Where?

Yeah, right in the stomach.

Do you feel that now?

Yeah, it's sore. . . .

Does it hurt a lot when you feel it?

Yeah.

Where did it get you, right here? (Probing the subject's stomach) Is this sore?

Right in there.

That's where they got you, right there. You only last a few minutes, huh?

Not even that. I just black out and that's it.

Can't you see the other people around you now?

No.

Can you see yourself lying there at all?

Yes, I can see myself laying there in the dirt.

You don't see any of the others?

No.

Can you see what they're doing to you afterward? Are they just letting you lie there, or what?

I don't know. I just float along.

Subject number two is a young woman who seems to recall a life as an English immigrant who came to the United States in 1856. As in so many regressions, the young woman experienced a sex reversal while remembering her former life as Philip Montgomery. Philip settled on a small farm in southern Virginia with his aunt and uncle. When Williams began the interview, Philip was ten years old.

Philip: I'm out chopping some wood. My aunt is washing clothes, and my uncle is out bringing us home some food supplies.

Williams: Where does he get those?

Philip: Well, it's a little place about nine, ten miles from here. It sells flour and other foodstuffs.

Williams: Do you have a farm?

Philip: Yeah, a small one. We're just starting to raise corn and a few other things.

Moving ahead ten years, Williams learned that Philip's aunt had died and that the two men were still eking out a meager living on the small farm. At the count of three, Williams progressed Philip ahead another ten years.

Philip: I'm in the village.

Williams: What village?

Philip: It's Hooversville, or something like that. I can't rightly remember. There isn't even a signpost coming into town. [Modern maps do not list a Hooversville, Virginia. There is, however, a Hornsbyville (population 200). At one point during the regression the entity said that he lived either in Virginia or "almost Virginia." Hoopersville, Maryland (population 150) lies just across Chesapeake Bay from Virginia.]

Hard times on the farm had forced Philip and his uncle to seek employment in the village. The uncle had become very ill, and Philip supported them by riding as a guard and a relief driver on the coachlines. Another ten years found Philip with a broken leg which he had suffered when he had gone to recover the body of his uncle, who had fallen over a cliff.

Williams: What was he doing falling off a cliff if he was so sick and in bed all the time?

Philip: I told you that he would get better once in a while. One day a bear started bothering things in the village, and all the people were out after him. There was a big bounty for him, so everyone was trying to get him. Stupid uncle went out after the bear and fell off the cliff!

How do you live?

Mrs. Jones next door comes over every morning and makes me get up out of bed.

Is she a widow?

No. She's got a husband.

How old are you now?

Forty-seven, I guess, or forty-eight.

How old is Mrs. Jones?

Hard telling.

I'm going to count to three and it will be ten years later. One, two, three. Now what are you doing?

I'm in the village getting ready to go on a trip with the stagecoach. This is going to be one of my last trips.

Why?

Because they make ya stop. I'm not that good of a shot.

Do you have to be a pretty good shot?

Oh, yeah. We got robbed once.

... I'm going to count to three and it will be ten years later. One, two, three. Now what are you doing?

Just laying down in the old bed.

Why, what's the matter?

I'm getting old and feeble, I guess.

How old are you?

Sixty or so.

You should be full of pep.

I'm not.

How do you live now?

Mrs. Jones comes over once in a while, or she sends her daughter over with some donuts and stuff.

How old is the daughter?

She's getting up somewhere like me, but not quite as old. Mrs. Jones is ready to hit the sack.

But you're not?

Can't tell. Maybe.

I will count to three and it will be ten years later. One, two, three. Now what are you doing?

Oh, I guess I'm sick, sicker than ever.

What's the matter?

I guess I'm really getting old.

How old are you?

Close to the eighties. I'm not sure. I've got aches and pains all over.

Where's Mrs. Jones?

She's six feet under.

How's her daughter?

I don't think I remember.

She doesn't come down to see you?

No.

Who does come to see you now?

The sheriff.

Are you good friends?

Yes.

Still living all alone by yourself?

I've got a dog now. He's about six years old. An old hound dog.

I'm going to count to three and it will be ten years later. One, two, three. Now what do you see?

Nothing. I don't see nothing. It feels darn good.

But you don't see anything?

I just see an old stone over there.

What does it say on the stone, or can't you read it?

It's got moss over it; it's old.

Are you dead?

I guess so.

How long have you been dead?

About eight years. Nine years.

Do you enjoy that?

Well, I don't know. I can't feel nothing, how can I enjoy it?

Do you ever see anyone by that stone?

Oh, yes.

Who do you see?

Mrs. Jones's daughter once in a while brings flowers. She's getting old, boy.

Did you ever try to talk to her?

No.

Why not?

'Cause I don't want to, I guess.

Have you ever seen your uncle?

Oh, I guess I saw him once.

What's he doing?

Oh, setting around just like me.

How does time pass here? Does it seem that time is going on?

It feels all right to float up and down.

Do you enjoy it?

Yeah!

Now I'm going to count to three and we will go back again to your last day in this life. One, two, three. Now what's happening?

I just don't feel so hot.

Why?

I ache all over.

How old are you?

I must be close to ninety.

Is anyone with you?

I'm all alone.

What are you doing, just lying in bed?

Yeah.

Now what's happening? Time is moving on a little bit.

The sheriff comes in. He brings me food. He looks at me and then runs out. Then this guy with the black suit comes in. There's two guys. One comes in, puts this thing on my stomach and it hurts. He has glasses on, and he shakes his head no. Then this other fellow, the minister of the peace or whatever you call him, he blesses himself or something.

Did they talk to you at all?

No, they didn't talk to me, they talked about me.

Did you talk to them?

No, how could I talk to them?

Why?

Dead.

Oh, you're already dead?

Yes.

How do you feel?

I feel all right.

What do they do to you?

Well, a lot of townpeople come around the house and say, 'oh, what happened?' Some say that I was a good rider.

What do they do with you?

They're taking me over to this place to fix me up.

How do they fix you up?

I don't really know. I guess they're doing something to me. Cleaning me up and stuff.

Now what are they going to do?

*Now they're putting some stuff on my face. I guess he's
painting it a reddish color. Then he puts me into this suit, I
guess. He puts this floppy thing down my shirt. He looks like
he's choking me with it.*

Can you feel it?

No.

Now what are they doing?

*Now they're putting me in this wooden box. It's a funny
shape. They shut it, put nails around it. People came after
that and put flowers around it.*

What did they do with the box then?

*The next day they picked it up, about six guys, and they
first put it in a carriage. Then they start walkin' with a bunch
of people behind them. Some folks wore black, and the
women were crying like babies and stuff. They got me up to
the old cemetery, way up past where I use' to live. They had
to walk umteen miles.*

Is Mrs. Jones's daughter there?

*Yes. She's just crying. They got me up there, these two old
guys, I guess, that got done digging a hole. I didn't know
what they wanted the hole for, but after a while I found out.
They put a guy in it. Put me in it, I guess it was! They said a
bunch of words.*

What did they say?

*I don't know, from dust to . . . an' all this stuff, and he says
to bow our heads in silent prayer, an' all this stuff.*

You're watching over them?

Oh, yeah.

Does it bother you to watch?

No. Why would it bother me? I don't feel anything.

Then what happens?

*After that some folks start walking away. Mrs. Jones's
daughter just sat there by the minister and she bawled her
head off. One brought a little box for that water in that little
hole. Now they're covering me up with dirt.*

Do you watch them now?

No.

What do you watch?

I don't know. I just going up in the clouds, I guess. I watch different people. I see people dying and watch people crying.

Do you watch their funerals?

Oh, half of it.

How come you don't watch all of it?

Because I don't like to.

Did you see Mrs. Jones's daughter after she died?

Oh, yes.

Did you get a good chance to talk to her?

No.

Why not?

I didn't want to.

Does she want to talk to you?

I guess so. I don't want to talk to her.

You just watch people?

Yes.

Time is going to go on a little farther, and it is a little while before you are born again. Did you decide on your own what time you are to be born again, or what?

I just don't understand what you just said.

Time goes on and then all of a sudden you're born again, aren't you?

I don't see that.

I will count to three and you will. One, two, three. Now you are born again, aren't you?

You mean into the life that I live now?

Yes.

Oh, I can see.

Let's go back six months to a year before birth. Tell me what you're doing and what you see?

I don't see nothing; I'm sleeping.

What made you decide to be born again? Did you have anything to say about that?

No, sir! I guess not.

What's the first thing you remember?

I don't remember nothing.

A little while ago you told us that you remembered.

Well, I didn't quite understand the first few minutes.

You don't remember anything before that?
No.
I'll count to three and we'll go back to six months before you were born. One, two, three. Now what do you see?
Nothing.
How do you feel?
Cooped up or something. [Is he describing the sensation of being confined to the womb?]
Let's go back another three months. One, two, three. Now what do you see?
Nothing. [Does the soul enter the body at six months? The subject felt "cooped up" at six months, but feels nothing at what would correspond to the third month of pregnancy.]
What do you feel?
Nothing.
Still looking around?
Oh, yeah, still up in the clouds. Boy, I see this funny thing going around. [At what would be the third month of his mother's pregnancy, the subject claims to be floating, "still up in the clouds."]
Do you ever think about coming back to earth?
I like it right where I am!
I'm going to count to three and you will be back to the present time and still sound asleep. One, two, three. You won't consciously remember any of what you have just said and to hear it won't bother you. What's your name?
Lois W - - -.
What's the date?
October 3, 1967.

Subject number three recalled what appeared to be a previous life as a telegrapher in the Confederate Army. When Williams moved the entity back to about the year 1400, subject number three told the hypnotist that he was a fourteen-year-old fisherboy who worked with his father along the coasts of England. Progressing the entity to the age of thirty, the subject told the hypnotist that he now had his own fishing boat and ran a tavern on land. He had prospered. But his traveling and his outdoor life had not proved to be an elixir which would prolong his life.

At forty, the personality told Williams that he was burning up with fever.

Wiliams: Is anyone helping you? Is there anyone doing anything for you?

Fisherman: No, I'm all alone . . . layin' on my bed. . . .

Williams: Let's go on a few hours. How do you feel now?

Fisherman: I don't feel nothing.

Williams: What's happened?

Fisherman: I think I'm dead now. I don't feel nothing.

Williams next brought this subject to the year 1900 and discovered an existence at that time, too. This aspect of subject number three's regression is currently under investigation and could prove to be a case as solid as that of the rebirth of Jonathan Powell. Certain specific facts, names, dates and place names were given, which, if substantiated, could establish the previous existence of Michael MacIntire. Here are some edited excerpts from this case-in-progress.

What year is it?

1910.

I'm going to count to three and it will be five years later, understand? One, two, three. What are you doing now?

Sailing.

Where?

United States. From England to the United States.

How old are you now?

Forty-five.

What year is it?

1915.

We will move along until you get to the United States. Now you're there. What do you see?

New York.

Are you going to live there?

Yeah.

We'll move along five years. I will count to three and it will be 1925, understand? One, two, three. What do you see now?

Nothing. [Williams had jumped past the death experience.]

What are you doing?

I can't remember.

I will count to three again and we'll go to your last day as Mike. One, two, three. Now what do you see?

People working.

Where?

Factory.

Where's this factory?

New York.

What are you doing?

I just made a machine; we're making machines.

Go on, tell us what happens this day. It's getting a little later in the day. What's happening now?

Someone robs the money.

What's the date?

The exact date?

Yes.

1925.

What month, what day? You saw the newspaper this morning before you came to work, didn't you? You can remember that and you can see the date right on it, can't you? Look at that date. What does it say?

(The subject gives the exact date.)

You say that someone "robbed the money" there? Tell us about it.

I go to try to stop him and he shoots me.

Where does he hit you?

In the heart.

Does that hurt?

Yes.

What do you feel?

Pain at first, then it eases. I'm dying.

We're going to go back an hour. You seem to have an English accent yet, don't you? Let's hear you say a few words. What's your name?

Mike. [The subject speaks with a pronounced accent. It is

rare for a regressed subject to assume a former accent or speak in a language foreign to that with which he is currently familiar.]

How old are you?

Fifty.

I'm going to bring you along now. You feel very good after they shot you. You have no more pain, right? I want you to drift along until you can tell me the next thing you see. You're going on and on. Now you're beginning to see something. What do you see? There is something there; tell me what you see.

Someone carrying me.

Where are you?

Factory.

Who's carrying you?

One of my friends.

Where are they carrying you?

To the doctor.

Are you still alive?

Yes.

Now you're with the doctor. What's happening?

I'm dead.

If we become convinced that there is no death, only change, then we must next ask ourselves what part of the divine plan is served by placing each individual human soul on such a cycle of rebirth. In *Dialogues on Metempsychosis* J. G. von Herder saw reincarnation as the same law of economy which rules throughout nature. The soul who has not become ripe in one life is put into the experience of living again until it is perfected. In its flesh life, Herder said, "... the soul lies captive in its dungeon, bound as with a sevenfold chain, and only through a strong grating, and only through a pair of light and air-holes can it breathe and see. . . ." But it is through such repeated sojourns on earth that God trains us for ". . . a complete divorce from the sense-life."

"Man is the result of his own past, being what he has made himself," wrote Olive Stevenson Howell (*Heredity and Reincarnation*). Miss Howell saw the differences which characterize people as the summed-up results of the experiences of previous lifetimes. "The birth of a genius, a saint, a sage, those remarkable differentiations from the average stock that so puzzle the observer of life, can thus easily be accounted for ... they are ... the product of accumulated endeavor and work carried over a period of many lives; they but reveal the finer possibilities and powers that lie dormant in others. In them is witnessed a flowering of the Spiritual Ego."

Some people may be troubled at the aspect of one's present life being a harvest of what he may have sown in a past life. The anxious will argue that such a philosophy would make one but a slave to the past, a past not even remembered. Dr. Theophile Pascal spoke to such an argument in *Reincarnation: A Study in Human Evolution*. If we are slaves of the past, Dr. Pascal assures us, we are masters of the future. "If fate compels us to reap what we have sown, we yet have the future in our hands, for we can tear up the weeds, and in their place sow useful plants. Just as, by means of physical hygiene, we can change within a few years the nature of the constituents that make up our bodies, so also, by a process of moral hygiene, we can purify our passions and then turn their strength in the direction of gold."

Subject number four is another case-in-progress. This particular regression has excited an historian to investigate the life recounted by the entity, who claims to have been a horse trainer for the Queen of England at the time of the American Revolution. Again, certain peculiarities of language and bits of knowledge have convinced at least one open-minded scholar that there may be more here than a psychological phenomenon. Here are excerpts from this subject's regression:

What do you see?
Fields, rolling fields with horses.
Who are you?
Ivan O'Connors.
Where do you live?
In Scotland.
Where in Scotland?
Lanark.
Take this piece of paper. Did you ever see a pen like that?
No.
What do you usually write with?
With a feather.
How old are you, Ivan?
Seventeen.
Do you go to school?
*Not now, but I used to attend school at a neighbor's
house.*
What did you learn there?
We used to learn to write.
What do you do for work?
Work in the stable.
Whose stable?
The Queen's stable.
Why does she have a stable in Scotland when she is Queen
of England?
The grasses are finer in Scotland.
And you work there?
Yes.
Who is the King?
I believe it is King George III.
What year is this?
1760.
What do you eat?
Goat's milk and bread.
What do you have when you get home from work?
Cheese and milk.
Is that all?
Yes.

You said you ate well.
We have a lot of what we have.
Do you have your own goats?
Yes.
Who milks those?
My mother.
(Ten years later) What are you doing now?
I am in Russia.
What are you doing in Russia?
With the Queen's horses.
I thought they were in Scotland.
There's an international meet and race in Russia.
What year is it?
1770.
Who is the reigning monarch in Russia?
Don't know.
What are you doing here?
I have two horses for the Queen.
Do you know why you were called Ivan?
My father was Scottish, my mother was Russian.
What was your mother's first name?
I don't know; Relena, I think.
How many countries are in this race?
Nine.
(Ten years later) What are you doing?
I'm in London.
What are you doing in London?
Queen's horses.
Same job?
Yes.
Do you ever see the Queen or King?
I seldom see the King, but I often see the Queen.
Is she a nice woman?
Yes, but very airy. When she comes to the barns I must show her the horses and speak of what they have been doing. She is more interested in their style.
In their style?

Yes. In the way their manes are braided, in the color of their blankets.

It is very much show, then?

Yes, very much.

Is she a nice looking woman?

Quite nice looking.

What does the King look like?

Well, I've never seen the King right up close. From a little ways away he has a beard. He wears very fancy clothes.

Have you seen any of the children, the Prince of Wales or any of the members of the family?

No. I've seen them with her at a distance, at some of the races; but they have not much interest in the horses.

What year is this?

1780.

And you are in London?

Yes.

Do you live in London?

Yes. I considered my home in Scotland until my mother died. Now I consider it in London.

Where do you live? Do you have a house?

Yes. On a farm at the course.

What is the name of this place where they have their races?

The Queen's Course is the name of the track. To us it's just the track, we call it; but to be honorable, we must say the Queen's Course.

Could you describe the bridle and reins used for the horses?

When they are racing or training?

When they are racing.

When they are racing the run, we use the finest grade of leather, smoothed down. The Queen's colors are red and blue with white trim, spotted in gold and silver.

What is the shape of the bit used?

It depends on the horse, how hard his mouth is. Each horse has a different bit.

In a hard mouth what kind of a bit do you use?

A ball ring.

What is that exactly?

A bit with a ball about as big around as your thumb in the middle, and there are rings that are attached to this ball. This hits the horse's tongue and makes him much easier to control.

Who decides what bit you are going to use?

I do.

What do you use on a gentle horse?

A straight steel bit, sometimes covered with leather.

What is the leather for?

To keep it from damaging his mouth.

Do you hear much talk in London now about the American War?

Yes.

What is going on over in America?

I know not too much, because I spend a lot of time with the horses. From what I know, in hearing from gossip that goes around, is that the colonists want America to themselves without the Mother Country to help her. I don't know the situation so I couldn't say whether it is right or wrong. I would dare say this, that the Queen wants as much or more than the colonists have to give.

What year is this now?

1780.

But there is a war going on?

Yes.

Have you ever talked to the Queen about this?

No. When she comes we just talk of the horses.

Would you like to go to the colonies?

Not really.

Why?

Because my life is horse racing, and I don't believe they have such a thing in the colonies.

You have a very good job anyway now, don't you?

Yes.

Are you married?

No.

How old are you now?

Thirty-seven.

How much does the Queen pay you?

She pays me on a yearly basis. Last year she gave me one hundred pounds and the finest colt in the stable.

What did you do with the colt?

The colt I am training to race, to be one of my own, but I barely have time for it with all of the Queen's horses.

How much help do you have?

I have twelve hired hands.

Then you actually don't have to do the work yourself?

I don't have much heavy work. I have to make most of the decisions on the horses, and their leg troubles I have to diagnose.

How do you diagnose the leg trouble?

It depends on the horse and what is bothering him and where it is bothering. I have to decide on the training of these horses, and how many miles and where they should go every day to keep them in muscles.

To keep them in muscles? (Historian: Yes, that's a very good phrase!)

Keeping their condition up. And their wind. Certain of the horses go two and a half miles in a race, and they need much speed and stamina, and they need all the chance that they can get.

What do you feed a horse in a day?

They get oats, barley, mixed with milk and vinegar.

What's the vinegar for?

It keeps them on their toes and keeps their coat shiny.

You put the vinegar in the milk?

No. Each thing goes into the feed separate.

What proportions do you mix for one horse?

We use our hands, so many fists full of this, and so many fists full of that, and then you pour in the milk. It's just what you'd call a dab in our terms.

How has your own health been these last five years?

Very well. I was injured by a horse and had trouble with my leg, but I was up and going in two weeks.

Did you ever have to have treatment by doctors?

No, the expense is too high.

What happened with your leg? Who took care of that?

Nobody took care of it. I put some horse liniment on it and let it go.

What happened? Did you get kicked?

No. The jockey was mounting him and he started to run off. He rose on his hind legs and came down on my leg.

(Ten years later) Now what are you doing, Ivan?

I own sixty-five horses.

How did you get to own sixty-five horses?

The Queen gave them to me.

Why did she do this?

She had trouble in the States and lost the war.

What do you mean by the States? Is this what you used to speak of as the colonies?

Yes. They are the States now.

Could not the Queen afford to keep the horses after the war?

She could afford to, but she did not have the interest any more.

Did she give them to you, or sell them to you, or what?

She signed the ownership papers over to me. She still pays the hired help and the feed bills. She says that I deserve it after all the years of being honorable to her stable.

That was a very wonderful, generous thing for her to do.

Yes, very much so.

Do you see much of her now?

Not as much as it used to be.

Is she as kind to other people as she has been to you?

No, they say not.

How is the King nowadays—how is his health?

I don't know. For all I know, the King could be dead. I've not seen him since before the war was over in the States. People do not speak of him, they speak of the Queen.

Did you ever hear anyone speaking about any problems he might have had with his health?

I heard rumors that he was expected to die of some

disease. Then I heard that he had his head cut off! But you can't believe anything. [At the close of his reign, King George III was hopelessly insane.]

How old are you now?

Forty-seven.

(Five years later) What are you doing, Ivan?

I have a fine white house in the bluegrass country of Kentucky.

What are you doing in Kentucky?

I have the horses that the Queen gave me. I have fine stock stallions and I am raising them.

Why did you go to America?

Because neither Scotland nor England has the fine grass that the horses thrive on that they have in Kentucky.

What year is this?

1795.

When did you go to America?

Four years ago.

How did you hear about this wonderful grass in Kentucky?

Because King Louis of France sent me to Kentucky to pick up a fine colt to bring back to France.

What year did King Louis send you to America?

1791. [Although the reader might at first think that Ivan is antedating the popularity of Kentucky's bluegrass horse country by at least fifty years, historians tell us that the breeding of racehorses has been a leading occupation in that section of Kentucky since the late 1700's.]

How did you get to know Louis? How well did you know him?

I did not know him at all. He came to see the horses that the Queen used to own. He was very impressed and told me that my horses looked fine. He offered me a fine sum of money to go and pick up this colt, and told me to look at the fine grass in Kentucky. [It is known that Louis XVI was more interested in horseback riding and hunting than he was in the public affairs of his country. He kept a rendezvous with Madame Guillotine on January 21, 1793.]

You mean that King Louis came to London?

Yes. France and England had been at war and on hard terms, but they let this stand aside and the King came for these talks and the Queen showed him the horses.

Who is now the head of the United States?

George Washington.

Are you satisfied with Kentucky? Does it come up to your expectations?

Very much so. Not many people have settled in Kentucky, I am much alone. I have no dealings with the government. From what I hear, the government is fine.

If you hear so little, how do you know that George Washington is President?

I don't know that for sure. When I first came I talked with Mr. Washington. He wished me the best of luck with my horse breeding.

How did you happen to meet him?

Because he knew about King Louis sending me over after the colt.

Where did you meet him?

Jamestown.

What did he look like?

Tall, stout man with a lot of class.

You say that you have a big house in Kentucky?

A house and many acres of meadowland.

How did you get this land?

I just settled on it.

(Ten years later) Now what are you doing?

I'm watching Tom work around the paddock.

Who is Tom?

The head man.

How many horses do you have?

One hundred and four.

How much help do you have here?

Nine men.

Are they slaves?

Not slaves at all. Eight are Negroes and one is a white man, and they are not slaves at all and they get paid very well.

How much do you pay them?
Twenty dollars a month, and they stay here.
How near are you to the nearest big town and what place
is it?
About forty miles from Lexington. It is to the east.
Have you married yet?
Yes.
What is her name?
Virginia Reeves.
How old are you now?
Fifty-seven.
How many years have you been married?
Four years.
How old is your wife?
Thirty-three.
Do you have any children yet?
We have three.
Three! Are they boys or girls?
Two boys and a girl.
What are their names?
Charles, Louis, and Elizabeth.
(Five years later) What are you doing?
Nothing. Everything is black.
We will go back to your last day. What are you doing,
Ivan?
It's late at night.
What year is this?
1811.
What date?
July.
What is happening?
*Light all over the place. The barn's on fire. The hired hand
and I rush to the barn. Twenty-four horses in the barn. We
got them all out except the end stall. The stallion is in there.
The foundation of the farm is in there. Had to get him out.
Charles went to the door.*
What Charles? Your son?
No. My man. He opened the door. Tried to bring the horse

*out. It struck him. He went down and I ran into the stall.
The straw began catching on fire. It wasn't any use. Charles
was dead. I grabbed the horse. He wouldn't move. The last I
saw was a hoof coming in my face, then fire all over.*

What did you see right after this happened? Look down
and see.

*In the meadow, up on the hill, I see my family and
Charles's family. They're standing just by a marker.*

What are they doing there?

Just crying. Honoring us.

Do the cases recounted in this chapter add weight to the
philosophy that there is no death, only change? Just as each
individual, in the final analysis, dies alone, so must each
individual interpret the import of these cases of hypnotic
regression to fit his own particular concept of things.

It was in *Parerga and Paralipomena* that Schopenhauer
made his oft-quoted remarks concerning reincarnation: "The
individuality disappears at death, but we lose nothing thereby; for it is only the manifestation of quite a different
Being—a Being ignorant of time, and, consequently, knowing neither life nor death. The loss of intellect is the Lethe
but for which the Will would remember the various
manifestations it has caused. When we die, we throw off our
individuality, like a worn-out garment, and rejoice because
we are about to receive a new and better one.

"Were an Asiatic to ask me for a definition of Europe, I
should be forced to answer him: It is that part of the world
which is haunted by the incredible delusion that man was
created out of nothing, and that his present birth is his first
entrance into life."

In support of Schopenhauer's assertion that the Asiatics
generally accept the doctrine of reincarnation, we could, of
course, quote from several thousand volumes and numerous
Oriental philosophers and masters, but this sententious sum-
mary of the dogma of rebirth by Chuang Tzu (circa 450 B.
C.) says it all: "Birth is not a beginning; death is not an
end."

CHAPTER VII

BIBLE BELT BRIDEY MURPHYS

On July 15, 1968, Bill Williams drove his pickup wagon with the camper attachment into our driveway in Decorah, Iowa. We had been corresponding and exchanging research materials for almost a year to the day that Bill arrived from New Hampshire, and we had both been looking forward to working together on in-field investigation.

"I'll just sleep in my camper," Bill said. "That way I won't bother you at all."

"We have a spare bedroom and the house is air conditioned," my wife told him. "I don't think you'll want to sleep out in this Iowa heat and humidity."

Bill had never faced an Iowa July. By midday he was happy to move his suitcase into our spare bedroom and leave the camper to our two sons, who received his permission to take overnight turns roughing it with their friends.

I had been receiving tapes from Bill throughout the past year, but he had brought some new sessions with him and I was eager to hear them.

We listened to the new tapes in silence. When Bill rose to punch the "off" button of the last reel, I looked up from the notes I had been taking. "Bill, I know that you were very skeptical about the validity of reincarnation when you began your research, and I have been prejudiced against such a thing since my earliest childhood. Could all of this simply be some imaginative faculty of the human mind? Now with Jonathan it has to be much more, whatever it is, because you were able to find so much substantiation for his existence. But could some of these other cases be due to some quirk of the mind rather than memories of other lives?"

"I've got thousands of feet of tape that are full of mind tricks and other bits of odd phenomena," Williams said. "I learned early in my research that prospective subjects should not be allowed to hear any other subject being regressed or even to hear the tapes of any regression before he himself is regressed.

"Once I had three subjects sitting side by side, waiting to be regressed. I was new at this, so I let them stay in the same room. Each of them simply added to the other's story. I produced a false regression that came in chapters.

"Then, too, sometimes if I have not succeeded in placing the subject in a deep enough trance, he simply free associates a fantastic regression. The mind is a strange and wonderful thing and we really don't know a whole lot about it.

"But now I kind of get a feeling when a subject is reliving a past life. The first and most obvious sign is when he begins to say, 'I'm doing this' or 'I'm doing that.' In other words, he is reliving the experience rather than watching it occur to someone else. It seems then that we have a memory at work rather than a fanciful job of storytelling. Then, too, the subject often undergoes a dramatic change of facial expression or seems to have literally become a different person.

"No, the tapes I sent you, Brad, are what I feel to be recollections, the memories of other lives."

"It's obvious that by now you firmly believe in the existence of the human soul, spirit, mind, psyche, call it what you will," I said. "What do you feel happens to the soul after physical death?"

Bill considered the question. "I think that there are several layers of consciousness," he said. "What we call physical life is only one layer—not necessarily the bottom one. These layers go up, up, up. I think that when one dies his soul will pass to a level of consciousness which is very closely related to our physical world. The soul there can still see what's going on in the physical world, and in some cases may be able to make contact with people who are in the physical world. Such instances may explain some 'ghost' phenomena and some spirit communication.

"I had one subject tell me that he could recall a period after the death experience in which he 'floated' above the graveyard and occasionally went into town to visit his brother's house. Several times he tried to make contact with his brother, but the man was never receptive. Once the subject said he mustered enough psychic strength to knock over a lamp in an attempt to attract attention, but he gave up when the cat got the blame.

"I believe that a soul remains on this lower level for varying lengths of time, depending on the manner in which he died. In my research I have found that those who died an early or a violent death tend to stay on this lower level longer than those who die of old age.

"The next step would seem to be what the entity describes merely as floating, being unable to see what's going on in the lower levels. Subjects always seem very calm at this level.

"A higher step, I would assume, is when the soul describes itself as doing nothing. This may be the final stage before rebirth; I don't know. All this is theory, of course."

"What about Karma, Bill?"

"Karma is difficult to pin down unless you know a lot about your subject's background and you are able to obtain the records of a good many regressions from the same subject. In those cases where I have known something of my subject's history or have been able to learn something of his background and have been able to get good detail on several of his past lives, I have seen a definite pattern of Karma being played out."

"So the divine laws of compensation, 'what ye sow, so shall ye reap,' do seem to be in effect," I commented.

"I believe so," Bill said. "Maybe Jesus wasn't trying to be so mystical as some interpreters of the Bible say he was. Maybe when he said that man must be born again, that's exactly what he meant. Just plain, 'you must be born again,' period. Likewise, his admonition to lay up treasures in heaven rather than on earth certainly becomes extremely meaningful in the dogma of Karma. The life you live on earth becomes your treasure, and the way you live your life is what counts, not how many wordly possessions you can accumulate."

"Do you feel," I asked, "that when Jesus told man to 'be perfect even as your Father in heaven is perfect,' he was referring to a spiritual progression in which one's spiritual lessons continue until the soul reaches the point where it can be absorbed into the Divine Mind? And what about Divine Mind? Do you believe in God?"

"If anything," Bill replied, "my research has strengthened my belief in God. I believe that God is a force that is *in* everything and a *part* of everything."

"Is this a benevolent force or do you see it as an impersonal force?"

"Both. It's an impersonal force because it isn't out to do any particular favors for any particular person, but it's a benevolent force because it knows no evil."

"Is there also an evil force?"

"Not in my opinion," Bill said. "Evil is a relative thing. There is no cold, only an absence of heat. There is no evil, only a lack of good. The reason that there is evil is because people don't allow the full expression of the God force in their lives. When we shut out this force we are left with evil."

"Bill, man—especially Western man—isn't particularly interested in a discussion of metaphysics. What do you think is the significance of your studies? You yourself are a practical man. Is there any practical application of your studies to the doctrine of reincarnation?"

"Probably not," Bill commented, "unless reincarnation can be proved to the satisfaction of everyone. My work provides me with personal satisfaction. Maybe it helps some people. And maybe someday I'll come up with a dozen cases as good as the case of Jonathan Powell—cases that everyone would believe, cases so concrete that no one can deny them."

"There are few people in our Judaeo-Christian culture who seem to realize that the majority of the world's religions do believe in reincarnation," I pointed out.

"And many believe in transmigration," Bill added.

"Have you found any evidence of transmigration in your research?" I asked. "Have you discovered anyone who claims to have been animal, fish, or fowl in a former life?"

"No." Bill shook his head. "Man always seems to be man."

"Do you see animals as having souls?"

"Possibly," Bill answered. "But they have their own levels. If they did not have something, why have so many people seen that ghost cat in our house?"

"Maybe," I speculated, "the ghost cat is within the memory of a ghost man."

Bill shrugged off my argument. "Then it would seem that someone would see that ghost man once in a while, too."

"Let's consider for a moment that this book should lead a good many people to undertake a serious study of reincarnation," I said. "Let's say that in another few decades reincarnation is established as fact. Do you feel that such a doctrine will offer a spiritual crutch to people? Will they think that they no longer have to worry about what they are doing in life, because they will have another chance in a future existence? Will the weaker breathren say, 'Well, I'll be reborn a hundred times and I can raise a little hell in this life and make it up in the next one'? Will the despondent commit suicide to escape the problems in their present life so that they can hurry on to the next one?"

Bill chuckled. "No, I don't think so. For one thing, a lot of people feel that way now. A lot of folks feel that they can go out and raise hell as long as they become contrite in their old age and make some expiation. If reincarnation should ever become well accepted in the Western world, I believe the Karma trend will begin to show through more and more.

"My personal belief is that nobody ever gains anything by suicide. The chief reason someone commits suicide is because he has a problem he feels he cannot face. In the dogma of reincarnation, one would come to realize that if he did not face his problem in this life, he would still have to face it in some other life. If anything, such a philosophy might decrease suicide. Once man has been made responsible for his actions and has been made to learn that he is going to have to come back to set his own road straight, he is going to want to face up to his problems and get them over with."

My wife bought us a fresh pitcher of lemonade. "I've called Rita and Rich Schmidt for tonight," she said. "They'll be able to make it."

"Good," I said, jotting down their names. "We have some volunteers coming tonight," I told Bill. "Rita is a student of the paranormal, and I guess she is what one would call a 'natural hypnotist.' She was quite adept at the ancient art of mesmerism as a young girl until her family doctor and the parish priest made her stop putting spells on her classmates and family."

"I don't think Rich is quite so enthusiastic," Marilyn said.

"Rich is a bit skeptical about the whole business," I admitted. "But he tries to keep an open mind, and he never does anything to discourage Rita from studying the field. I doubt if he'll let you hypnotize him, however."

Bill shrugged. "One subject a night is good. If we can have one a night for the next week, and if we have even one good one, it will have been worth my trip."

That night, after the children were in bed and the Schmidts had entrusted their sons and home to a babysitter, we were ready to begin experiment number one. Rita asked that no one be present while Bill placed her under hypnosis, so Rich and Marilyn waited downstairs. I checked the tape recorders, adjusted the lights, saw to it that Rita was comfortable.

"I'll wait downstairs with the others," I told her then. "Bill, you can call down when she's under."

I was not halfway down the stairs when I heard Bill's voice: "Okay, she's in trance."

Bill admits that a good deal of the hypnotist's prowess lies in his reputation. It is something like being the fastest draw in the West. A majority of people are "psyched out" just by the thought of his legendary abilities with a six-shooter. So it is with being a widely known hypnotist. Once, in a demonstration, Bill told a group of twenty junior high school students that he would place them in trance simply by willing it. There would be no look-me-in-the-eye business, he told them. He would just "think" them to sleep. Bill turned his back on the young people and, although he was thinking about something far removed from the experiment on the stage, seventeen of the twenty boys and girls went into a light trance state. Power of suggestion and belief in the hypnotist's "magic" certainly have a great deal to do with one's ability as a hypnotist.

Bill took Rita back through various stages in her development and had her write the alphabet at different age levels. It was remarkable to observe a reversal of handwriting from the careful flow of a twenty-seven-year-old woman to the childish scrawl of a six-year-old schoolgirl.

Rita had been placed successfully in a deep trance. Now Bill wanted to try for the birth experience. Rita recalled a bed . . . a big bed. . . .

How old are you?

Couple of days.

What have you got on for clothes?

Diaper and a little top.

Any people around?

Yes.

Who's there?

Mmm, my little sister. [Rita has a twin sister.] *I'm just layin' there.*

Is your mother there?

Hm-mmm. (She nods.)

What is she doing?

Oh, she looks like she's happy.

All three of you are in the bed together?
Hm-mmm. (She nods.)
Is this the first thing you remember?
(She nods.)
How do you feel?
I don't know.
Do you feel tired?
I'm hungry.
You're hungry? Are you always hungry?
Hm-mmm. (She nods vigorously.)
Bill deemed the regression to childbirth to be successful.

"Now, at the count of three," he told Rita, "you will go back before you were born. Back to another time. You will go back until you remember being someone else. It may be fifty years; it may be a hundred years. You are going back. Farther and farther back. One, going back; two, farther and farther back; three . . . what do you see now?"

In a tremulous voice, Rita described a country road. "I'm walking, trying to get away. The cart is getting closer . . . closer. . . ." Rita bursts into tears of anguish.

Bill said, "There's no need to cry. There is no pain. No fear. I'll count to three and you'll be right back at the present time. You'll be wide awake and feeling better than you have felt for a long, long time."

Bill's first concern is for his subject. Whenever a traumatic scene occurs, Williams is there to guide the subject through the experience or, if the condition worsens, to extricate the subject completely and bring him back to the present. It might make for a good case study and a dandy tape recording to allow the subject to thrash about and scream through the death throes, but such an experience could also dredge up long-buried memories which were best left dormant.

"Will you try to regress her again?" I asked.

"Not tonight," Bill said, shaking his head. "We evidently hit a very emotional incident, and I don't want to send her back there so soon. But she is such a good subject that I would like to see what kind of a traveler she would make."

In another phase of his research with hypnosis and the paranormal, Williams has been seeking out subjects who are particularly good at astral projection, that mysterious facet of mind which enables some individuals to free their psyches from their physical bodies to wander outside the barriers of time and space. Bill has been experimenting with out-of-body travel in the area of medical diagnosis and has achieved some remarkable results. He pointed at Rita and told her to fall into a deep sleep, and she once again went into a trance.

"Where shall we send her?" he asked me.

"How about sending her to the home of our editor?"

"Good idea," Bill agreed. "Do you have his home address?"

I got my address book and pointed to the appropriate listing.

"Rita, you are now going to travel through space and visit the home of a friend of ours who will be the editor of our book. He lives at [complete address]. You're traveling over Iowa, Indiana. Look down at the fields, the lights. And now you're approaching New York City. Have you ever been there before? (She shakes her head no.) Look below you. There's Times Square. The Empire State Building. Now go to his address. Do you have it?"

Rita gave a brief description of our editor's home and when Bill told her to see our friend in "X-ray form," she looked upon him diagnostically. The old injuries and present-day health conditions which Rita saw were later verified through a long distance telephone call. It is true that my editor and I have worked closely together for three years, on the other hand, we have never discussed matters of personal health.

"Where shall we send her now?" Williams wanted to know.

"Dave and Jean just had a baby in Niagara Falls, Canada," my wife said. "Let's see if Rita can tell us how mother and child are doing."

Rita described the falls by night (she had never been there), described the home of our friends in great detail, and told us things about the baby and recent developments in the home which we were later able to verify by letter and telephone.

"I never get to travel anywhere in person," Rich complained after his wife had been awakened. "Maybe I can get around that way. I'd like to have you hypnotize me!"

"You're going to volunteer?" I asked Rich.

"You bet," he said, taking the chair which his wife had just vacated.

But here another mystery of hypnosis entered the scene. Just as not everyone can become a good hypnotist, so it is that not everyone can be hypnotized. Rich was not fighting Bill's will. He had become intrigued with the whole business and he *wanted* to be hypnotized. We were to see evidence of this phenomena more than once during our week of intensive research.

On the other hand, my wife decided to volunteer, but doubted that she could be hypnotized. It took less than a minute to place her into deep trance.

We watched Marilyn regress from thirty-year-old mother of four to confident five-year-old boasting how well she knew her ABC's. Her handwriting deteriorated from its normal neatness to the four-inch-high letters of her kindergarten days. Her birth experience was most interesting.

I'm going to count to three and you are going right back to your first day, the day you were born. You are going to see things very clearly and remember everything. One, two, three. Now what do you see?

Nothing.

What do you feel?

Nothing. [It is the day she was born, but it may be prebirth.]

I'll count to three and you will be just a little older. Tell us the first thing you feel. One, two, three. Now what are you doing?

I'm not sure.

It should be coming clearer now.

I guess it is a nurse.
What is she doing?
Walking with a baby.
Where are you? I'll count to three and it will be very clear. One, two, three. Now what are you doing?
I'm crying.
What is the matter?
I want to be held.
How big are you?
Just itsy.
Do you see your mother?
No. I'm in a nursery.
I'm going to count to three and it will be two weeks later. One, two, three. Now what are you doing?
I'm still in the nursery.
You're still in the nursery? In the hospital?
I guess so. I can see around me.
How old are you?
I don't know. I'm getting stronger.
What is your name?
I don't think I have any; I'm "baby." [Marilyn is an adopted child.]
Just "baby"? All right, I'm going to count to three and it will be one week later. Now what are you doing?
In my bed. On my back. First time.
What do you mean, first time?
They never turn me on my back.
Oh? Do you like it better on your back?
I can see around.
Oh! What do you see?
People walking around.
Where is your mother?
I don't know.
Let's go to the first time you see Mother. Someone you know is Mother. Let's go to that time. When I count to three you will be with Mother. What do you see?
Pretty smile.
What does Father look like?

Dark hair. Pretty smile.
What does Mother look like?
Dark hair. Kind of heavy. Tears.
Why does she have tears?
She's happy.
Do you have a name now?
(Crying) *Marilyn.*
Can you see other people around?
Oh, yeah. Lot of them. (She names several relatives.)
Why did it take so long to have a mother?
My mama didn't like me. She didn't want me.
This mother likes you, doesn't she? She loves you.
She's smiling. She's got tears. They're all smiling. They are all crying.
You must be very happy now. . . .
Oh, yes!
All right. I'm going to count to three. . . .

As an interesting footnote to Marilyn's regression to the birth experience, a ten-year study by Dr. David M. Cheek, President of the American Society of Clinical Hypnosis, indicates that newborn babies are much more aware of their immediate environment than previously had been supposed. During the course of the decade of his study, Dr. Cheek examined eighteen women and three men who knew their adoption history. Babies are usually taken out of the delivery room immediately in order to spare the mother any anguish, but Dr. Cheek found that the babies slated for adoption had a keen awareness of their rejection. The results of the study can be briefly summarized as follows:

1.) Newborn babies need to hear their mothers talking about them immediately after delivery. Such soothing vocal reassurance is usually denied babies up for adoption because either the anesthesia prevents their mothers from speaking to them or else they are hurried from the room to the nursery within moments after birth.

2.) Babies who heard their mothers weeping during or

immediately after delivery were left with feelings of guilt for having caused their mothers such pain.

3.) All babies, both adopted and unadopted, recall feelings of acceptance when placed in a general nursery. It appears that some sort of communication goes on among babies who are kept together. Age-regressed subjects also remembered kind words from the nurses and the touch of gentle hands.

4.) Those babies placed in foster homes before their final adoption accumulate a great deal of resentment because of the double adjustment which they are forced to make from natural mother to foster parents to adopting parents.

To quote from *Clinical Hypnotherapy:* "We previously held the bias that newborn babies have insufficient development of their nervous system to allow storage of visual and auditory perceptions from the first moments of life. Their initial experiences pointing to the possibility of keen awareness at birth were thought to be accidental. When volunteer information accumulated we then learned how to search for information included in these reports. Subsequently we became convinced that there is a definite memory of birth in the subconscious portion of the mind which can be recalled with hypnotic age-regression. . . ."

After Marilyn's age-regression to the birth experience, Bill brought her back to the present to allow her to take a brief rest. Then at his command of "deep sleep," Marilyn went back . . . farther and farther back. . . . ("It was like I was traveling through space," she told me later. "I seemed to be floating . . . but that denotes a kind of lazy travel. This was like traveling a thousand miles a second through open sky or space. I seemed weightless, bodiless. . . .")

Williams: What do you see now?

Marilyn: Sand . . . camels . . . I'm on my mother's lap on a donkey. . . .

Marilyn described a life of extreme poverty and a bleak nomadic existence. When Williams asked her what color her robe was, she replied: "What's color?" When asked to draw the pitcher she was filling with water, she did not know what to do with pen and paper. "Have you ever drawn something with a stick in the sand?" Williams asked her. She nodded her head. "Then pretend this [pen] is a stick and this [paper] is the sand." Marilyn drew a crude but recognizable sketch of a typical Mideastern water pot.

In a lifetime which seemed to have terminated but a few years before her present birthdate, she again lived in squalor in an adobe hut by the ocean in what appeared to be a description of the Gulf of Mexico. She had but one dress and survived on the most meager rations until she finally starved to death.

Imagination? If it was, it was a most surprising display. If Marilyn had been indulging in psychic play-acting, I would have expected her to envision herself as a diva enslaving the masses through the spell of an operatic aria, a lady-in-waiting to the Queen of some medieval court, or at least something as romantic as a female trapeze artist. But sand ... a nomad's tent ... an adobe hut ... a bleak, colorless existence? My wife knows what colors are in this life, as any visitor to our home can testify. And as a proficient and industrious seamstress, she sees to it that she and her daughters are well dressed. No, if it were some fanciful flight of the psyche, the lives it chose to mime would seem to be decidedly out of character.

"Perhaps this is a Karmic pattern," I teased her. "You must really have lived it up in an early life to have had to struggle through such miserable existences in those two more recent lives. At least now, in this life, you are being compensated and are most certainly moving rapidly forward in your spiritual evolution."

"On the contrary." Bill chuckled. "Maybe this is the life in which she is really working off her Karmic debt, by being married to a writer. If she carries off this life she may be able to wash her slate of debts clean."

"What about Karma?" Marilyn asked, still puzzling over what she had heard of her alleged former lives during the playback of her regression. "Do you really believe in it, Bill?"

Rich spoke up. "First of all, what the heck is this Karma you've been talking about?"

"Karma is an ancient ethical concept that holds that all of the actions which man performs on earth during his present existence, whether good or bad, determine what kind of life pattern he'll have in his future incarnation."

"You mean," Rich asked, "that an ax-murderer in one life might end up being a murder victim in the next life?"

"Something like that," Bill said. "Basically, it's that ancient law of compensation mixed together in equal parts with 'What ye sow, so shall ye reap.' "

"This afternoon you mentioned that you had been able to see patterns of Karma in certain cases which you've researched," I reminded Bill. "Can you illustrate the ethics of Karma by quoting from your own work?"

"Well, there was this one case which concerned a boy who, when regressed to about 1870, described a life of crime and violence. He lived in the West, and even as a teenager made his living by theft and robbery. When he was twenty-one, he and a companion staged a bank robbery during which someone was killed. He was caught, tried and hanged for the murder and robbery."

"His present life seems to comprise a perfect Karmic retribution for this past life of lust and violence. He was born of a married woman who was so indiscreet in her extramarital affairs that she did not even know who his father was. Her husband left her because of this pregnancy. There were older children in the family, who, when the father left, were put in orphanages and foster homes, as was the baby.

"After several years of institutional life, he was put into a foster home with his half-brother and sister. At about this time, the father of his half-brother and sister began to visit them. He began to treat the boy as his own son. He brought the boy gifts and gave him a father's companionship. For the first time the child began to feel wanted and loved. Then his life was shattered when the man died of a heart attack. His foster parents were good to him, but they could not replace the love which the father of his half-brother and sister had given him.

"The boy began to shift his love to his half-brother. He was starting to adjust after the father's death, when his brother was killed in an accident. Once again his life was shaken by being violently robbed of someone he loved. In the previous life he had sown the seeds of violent death as he robbed people of their possessions. In this life he has reaped the issue of this seed by being continually robbed of the person he loves.

"In a second case from my own research, a subject claimed a previous life as a governess in France in about the year 1800. In that capacity she managed to meet and marry a wealthy older man. She was very selfish and obsessed by money, jewels, servants and power. She devoted many years to making her elderly husband just as miserable as possible, and she was delighted when he finally died and left her in control of the property and money.

"She was a tyrant in dealing with her servants, so much so, in fact, that she was finally murdered by one of her maids, who refused to be so thoroughly demeaned. This woman's present life has strongly borne out the Karma concept. The youngest of several girls, she was born into a very poor family. She was brought up with little money or luxuries. For some unexplainable reason, her mother and her sisters abused her.

"One of her sisters told me, 'Poor Gloria spent her childhood crying. I don't know why, but we were always so mean to her. Even when she was a teenager there seemed to be an unspoken household conspiracy to give her the dirtiest jobs and to make her life miserable.'

"It seems that this woman was receiving from everyone in this life the same treatment she had dealt to others in the previous life experience."

"The poor woman," my wife commiserated. "Would she be doomed to being a scapegoat forever?"

"That's an interesting point about Karma, too," Williams replied. "When this girl grew up she was able to adjust emotionally and her family attitude changed. She is now quite well-adjusted and happily married. It was then that I met her. Her married sister is a friend of mine and one night I was playing some tapes at her house. Gloria was there and became interested in hypnotic regression. She volunteered to be a subject, and when I regressed her to her high school days she began to sniffle and whine. The younger I regressed her the more she began to cry. That's when her sister mentioned that she had always cried and that they had been cruel to her. I took Gloria back to the birth experience and beyond, and we learned of her previous existence as a sadistic mistress.

"Anyway, to get back to the Karma concept, one seems to have the opportunity to overcome, or to adjust, to the conditions into which he is born. If he makes a successful adjustment and improves his status through right living, there will be a corresponding improvement in the conditions into which he is born the next time. In some cases, like that of Gloria, one begins to reap the harvest of his adjustment in the present life."

On the next evening William Howard and his wife Virginia came over to the house to offer their services as subjects. Howard is an accomplished graphoanalyst who has begun a study of hypnosis. He was a willing subject and tried his best to cooperate, but he seemed to be more interested in studying Bill Williams' technique. Bill did succeed in placing Howard in a light trance state and regressed him to the time he was in high school and on the debating society. We were able to hear Howard repeat the summation which had won a crucial debate more than twenty years ago, but Howard would not budge beyond the birth experience. The same was true in the case of Virginia. She, too, could not be regressed beyond the first days after her birth.

The third night of Bill's stay in Iowa also produced a strikeout. A young writer friend of mine called to say that he would volunteer to serve as a subject. He had always been curious about hypnosis, and he speculated, "If I can remember a previous life of a couple hundred years ago, it might help me write a historical novel."

Bill could not even induce a light trance state in Mitchell, however. The young man sprawled in an easy chair, took off his shoes, did everything he could to make himself comfortable and cooperative, but there was no mind-traveling or age-regression for him.

"Who's set for tonight?" Bill asked, as we were setting up our tape recorders and readying the study on the fourth evening.

"A tough cookie," I warned him. "Don keeps an open mind about such matters, but I really feel that he will be impossible to hypnotize. William Howard and Mitch were trying to cooperate and they didn't go under. I'm afraid that Don, at least subconsciously, will fight you."

"That doesn't always matter," Bill said. "You know, it is as great a puzzle to determine who makes a good hypnotic subject as it is to figure out why some people make good hypnotists. Maybe Howard and Mitch were trying too hard to be hypnotized. Who is going to make a good subject is something a person just cannot judge ahead of time. That's part of the challenge of this research. When I begin with a subject before me, I never know if he will fail to respond in any manner whatsoever or if he will be another Jonathan Powell."

When Don sat down in the easy chair in front of Bill that night, I fully expected to see the hypnotist work diligently for twenty minutes or so before he declared another miss. I was amazed to see Don go into deep trance in about twenty seconds! The story he told us while regressed to what appears to have been another life experience is still being checked. Certain names he gave as the personality "Johnny Johnson" have been found in old records, and other aged deeds and registrations are presently being researched.

(In 1852, Johnny is first picked up as a miner in Colorado. He details coming West after a stay in Zanesville, Ohio, but he gives his parents' home as Rome, New York. Census statistics are spotty for 1822, the year of his birth, but records of Johnny's possible mother-to-be have been found. The fact that the woman's maiden name and her first name are a bit uncommon for the area and the time make this piece of preliminary research seem to have been fruitful and suggestive that additional investigation be carried out. Here are excerpts from the transcript of Johnny Johnson, hired gunman:

Can you read and write?

I can write my names.

Well, let's see you do it. Write on here. That's a pretty good signature.

Huh-huh. [Without providing him with any details whatsoever, I gave William Howard samples of the handwriting of "Johnny Johnson" and Don, the subject. The graphoanalyst pronounced the samples to have come from two entirely different personality types. Johnny's handwriting was analyzed as being that of a cold, cruel, dispassionate man. "Capable of murder?" I asked. "Without hesitation," Howard answered.]

I'm going to count to three and it will be ten years later. Now what are you doing?

Civil War.

Which army are you in?

Rebel.

How did you happen to join the Rebel Army when you are from New York?

I was in Texas.

What year is this?

1862.

Where are you now?

Somewhere in Tennessee.

What is the regiment?

Quantrill's.

Quantrill. No particular regiment? Just a. . . .

Guerrillas. (Quantrill's raiders were mustered into regular Confederate service late in 1862, but they continued to operate as an independent unit.)

What have you been doing?
Killing people.
Do you have any rank?
Boss.
They didn't call them sergeants or anything?
No.
This isn't really part of the Confederate Army, is it?
We're soldiers.
But you aren't associated with Lee or any of the others, are you?
We don't wear uniforms.
But you consider yourselves soldiers?
Yes, we get killed just like the regular soldiers.
Lot of your friends get killed?
Man, you don't have any friends in this outfit!
Why, is it a pretty tough bunch? Every man for himself?
That's the way it is.
Well, you are in Tennessee. What part of Tennessee?
Kingsport.
What have you been doing there?
Lookin' the town over.
Have they had any raids there?
No.
Planning any?
Just thinking.
This is 1862, you say. What month and day—do you know?
Summer.
We will drift in time until you decide what you are going to do in Kingsport. One, two, three.
Standing on the corner.
Doing what?
Thinking about robbing the bank.
Isn't Tennessee in the Confederacy?
Huh-huh. (Yes)
Why would you rob a Confederate bank?
Money.
So if you rob the bank you will do it on your own.

Right.

I see. Well, what do you think about robbing this bank? Do you think it would be worthwhile?

I doubt it.

Let's go on and see what you do. It's now a little bit later. How about the bank? Did you rob it?

No, I decided I couldn't get away.

What kind of pistol do you have?

Colt Navy.

How long is the barrel?

About eight inches.

What caliber is this pistol?

Forty-four.

How do you load the pistol? Do you carry cartridges, or what do you do for ammunition? (Johnny describes and goes through the motions of loading a cap and ball revolver.)

I'll count to three and it will be one year later. Now what are you doing?

On a horse.

Where?

West Texas.

Did you leave Quantrill back in Tennessee? Did you get tired of the raids, or what?

Just wanted to go West, man.

Aren't you worried about Quantrill's catching up with you and getting you?

Screw Quantrill!

What are you doing now?

Drifting.

Do you have anything definite in mind?

Nope.

Let's move along until you get settled down somewhere. Now where are you?

Mexico.

Where in Mexico?

Matamoros.

Quite a city, isn't it?

Yeah! (Ribald laughter)

You get around pretty well?

As well as I can!

What are you doing now?

Just hangin' around the saloons.

The slums are real slums too, aren't they? [Johnny has slurred the word "saloon" and Bill misinterprets it as "slums."]

Saloons!

Oh, I thought you said slums. What are you drinking?

Tequila.

What do they charge you for a shot?

I charge it.

Charge it and don't pay for it?

They think I'm going to pay for it!

What are you going to do for work, or aren't you going to work?

I don't know yet. I've got my gun.

Have you had to use it much?

When you are in Mexico you use one.

When was the last time you used it?

Out in Texas.

You say you had to use your gun in Texas. What happened?

Argument.

Over what?

I don't know. I was drunk.

What happened?

He shouldn't have drew on me.

Are you pretty fast?

I don't know. Fast enough.

How many men have you killed?

I don't keep track.

I am going to count to three again and it will be five years later.

Now what do you see?

California.

How did you happen to leave Mexico?

I was run out.

You didn't pay your bar bills?

I got in an argument and killed a couple of men.

How old are you now, John?

Too damned old.

What year is this?

It is about 1872 now.

That makes you pretty near fifty, doesn't it?

Somewhere in there.

Do you feel your age?

Uh-huh.

Are you still using your gun?

If I have to. But all that's about ended now.

Do you think you are going to settle down out here?

I don't know.

Don't you kind of miss Mexico?

Not a hell of a lot.

Can you make a living here? What do you do?

Work in a gambling hall.

In the games, or what?

I just stand around and keep order.

Bouncer?

No, I'm the gunman.

Do you ever have to use your gun?

Not anymore. Too much trouble. Too much law nowadays.

You just scare them a little, eh?

Just hit them over the head with somethin'.

Now it's five years later. What are you doing?

Nothing.

Where are you?

I don't know.

Are you alive?

No.

I am going to count to three and we will go back to your last day as John. What are you doing, John?

Layin' in bed.

What is the matter?

Sick.

What year is this?

It is about 187 . . . about 1877 or '78.
What month?
I don't know.
What is the matter?
Fever.
What kind of a fever?
I don't know.
How long have you had it?
Off and on since the war.
I see. How are you feeling now?
Terrible.
Let us go on in time a little and see what happens. A little
later now. Let's see what happens.
Nothing.
What are you doing?
Nothing.
What happened?
I died.
What did they do with your body? Can you see that?
Buried it.
Could you see your body when they were taking care of it?
What were they doing? Who was there?
No one.
Who took care of it?
Undertaker.
Where did they bury it?
Up on the hill.
You watched all that? Any friends there?
I didn't have any.
Oh. Then what did you do when they buried your body?
Just floated up above and watched them for a while.

When Carl volunteered to serve as a subject he did so with
the condition that he get to look "that hypnotist fellow over
good first."

"Now what about this hypnotism business," he said to Bill.
"Is there a possibility that if you put me under I won't come
back?"

"No, not unless you drop dead of a heart attack during the process," Bill told him.

"Well, let's say *you* had the heart attack," Carl countered. "Do I get lost in trance for the rest of my life?"

"If that should ever happen, you would simply awaken after a period of time just as you would from normal sleep," Bill answered.

"As long as you're already being interrogated by Carl, Bill," I said, "do you feel that it is possible for a hypnotist to make a subject commit some act which would be morally repugnant to the subject?"

"It is unlikely," Bill answered, "but I wouldn't say that it was impossible. If you wanted someone to rob a bank for you, you could probably hypnotize him and then condition him over a long period of time. You would not permit him to remember certain things you told him and you could suggest that his memory emphasize certain other bits of information you fed him. You could tell him that such-and-such a bank was really stealing from the people and that it deserved to be robbed. You could even condition your subject to believe that it was good and morally right to rob banks. But this would be a complex job."

"But you feel it would be possible to make some otherwise moral person commit a morally reprehensible act?" Carl asked.

"I think that it can be done, but the hypnotist would have to remake the subject's personality. Don't worry, Carl," Bill teased, "we don't have that much time tonight!"

"In reality, then, stories like *The Manchurian Candidate*, wherein a subject is programmed to become an assassin of the President of the United States, could really be made to happen," I said.

"Given the proper amount of time," Bill agreed. "Some crooked hypnotist couldn't say to himself, well, let's see, I'd like to rob a bank, but I don't want to do it myself so I'll hypnotize a subject to do it tonight while I set up a good alibi for my own whereabouts. Unless he happened to pick a subject whose basic nature happened to be that of a thief, the subject would probably not do anything contrary to his basic nature on the basis of one hypnotic trance and one post-hypnotic suggestion."

"What about the classic tale of the hypnotist putting some frail wench in his power and making her his sexual slave?" I asked. "Would it also be quite possible to take a prim and proper young miss and condition her to seduction over a period of time?"

"Isn't that what seduction is, anyway," Bill said, "the power of suggestion applied strategically and artfully over a period of time?"

"What about on-the-spot seduction during a trance?" Carl asked.

"Unless the woman were so disposed, she would probably wake up the moment the hypnotist phrased any question which she found personally offensive," Bill answered. "Whenever I do any therapy work with a woman, I always make it a point to have someone else around. Not because I'm going to do anything to her, but I know of cases in which women have created fantasies about themselves and the hypnotist *after* hypnosis."

"The thing I'm most worried about," Carl said, "is that hypnosis might in some way damage me psychologically. I've heard some pretty hairy things about these post-hypnotic suggestions."

"This is where the amateur parlor hypnotists and the supper club entertainment hypnotists have given hypnosis a bad name," Bill said. "Hypnosis is not to be taken lightly and it certainly is not to be used solely for the purpose of entertainment. The hypnotist has to have a great deal of common sense and take what he is doing very seriously."

"Carl," I remarked, "I have never seen Bill make any kind of suggestion which might make the subject appear foolish or which might in any way prove to be psychologically harmful to the subject. The subjects whom I have observed have come out of trance feeling refreshed both physically and mentally."

"I've more important things to do with hypnosis than to

play around with it," Bill added. "Well, Carl, shall we give it a try?"

In spite of his reservations, Carl proved to be a good subject. In his first regression beyond the birth experience of this life, Carl appeared to relive an existence as Tom Berneat, a Georgian, who enlisted to "fight Injuns" in 1851. Tom liked to draw, and effortlessly drew us some pictures and signed them—all with his right hand, although Carl is left-handed. We followed Tom's career as a pony soldier through the Civil War until, in 1871, somewhere in Utah. . . .

I hurt too bad.

What happened? Where does it hurt?

My chest.

I'll stroke your chest and then it won't hurt. Now you can talk. It doesn't hurt now, does it?

No.

What happened? What is going on?

We have been doing a powerful hell of a lot of fighting!

I'm going to count to three and then it will be all over with. Now what are you doing?

(Grunts)

Can you see your body there?

Yeah.

What are they doing with it?

Laying it on a big flat rock.

Where are the other soldiers?

Most of them are dead. They are picking them up.

Who is picking them up?

Couple of old troopers.

Have they picked you up?

No.

Let's go along until they do. Are they there yet? What do they do with you?

Putting my body in a hole.

Are you the only one in the hole or are there more there?

No, there are more there.

One big grave, eh?

Me in one hole and they are in another hole.

Do you have a big hole to yourself?

Yup.

How many are there?

Five of us.

What are you doing, just watching? Doesn't it bother you?

No.

Do you feel comfortable?

Yeah.

I'll count to three and what do you see? Are you still watching the soldiers?

Nobody there.

Are you watching your body? Do you stay there all the time?

Just standing there.

You are just standing there beside the grave. How long do you do this?

I don't know. Just stand there with the cross.

I am going to count to three and you will go back maybe a thousand years.

There is something around my neck.

What is around your neck?

(Pause) *It's like a . . . too tight. . . .* (Gasp)

It is too tight to speak easily? Let me loosen it up just a little; now you can speak easier. What are you doing?

I'm afraid. Big blocks. All day, all night, no water.

Would you like a drink of water so you can speak better? You probably haven't had water for quite a while. Just take a little sip. There. Now.

Move big blocks.

Where are these blocks?

All I know is, I move blocks.

How long have you been doing this?

I don't know.

How old are you?

I don't know.

Do you have a name?

I don't know. They call me "slave."

You have been doing this as long as you can remember?

Yeah.

What color is your skin?

Darkish red. [Carl seems to be describing a life as a Central American Indian who became enslaved by the Spanish Conquistadores.]

Dark red. How about the people who make you work?

We can't look at them. When we get beat, they put us in caves nighttime. Nothin' to eat.

What do you eat?

Piece of bread. Some soupy lookin' ... tastes like ... sweat.

How tall are you?

Fifteen or sixteen hands. I put my hands at my feet and count up.

I am going to count to three and we are going to go back ten years. Now what are you doing?

I don't know. There is something comin' at me. Real hairy.

Where are you?

(Excited, ignoring Bill's question) *My brother! They been pickin' people up, beating them up and taking them away.*

Who has been doing this?

People. Dressed up. Horses.

Where do they come from?

I don't know.

What do you have on for clothes?

Wear somethin' around my bottom.

Is that what everybody wears?

Yup.

What do the girls wear?

Long robes. Some don't wear nothing.

Are you grown up? As big as the men in the village?

No. I kinda funny.

What do you do that they laugh at?

Make funny faces and throw rocks at people.

What about your brother? Does he act the same way?

No. He pulls me down and keeps me from doing it.

Is he bigger than you?

Oh, yeah.

Do you have a mother and father there?

Oh, a daddy like me.

Does he make faces, too?

Yeah.

Let's count to three and see what you're doing one year later.

Looking at big things. Big square rocks.

Have you got something around your neck? Is it too tight? You have trouble talking? Let me loosen it.

My mouth is cut.

How did it get cut?

My face is cut, too. Big blocks. They put us there.

Who put you there?

Big men on horses dragged us with ropes and hurt us and beat us. I made faces and they don't like us.

What did they hit you with?

Some long thing they swing and snap.

Did they capture women and girls, too?

They have been making my mom carry water and wash and carry more water. They take everybody. They make us cut trees, put coals on the big rocks, make warm coals, push big rocks.

I am going to count to three and you are going to your last day.

They have a big circle. Men on horses lined up and down with spears, helmets. Silver shines, and they are running at us. We are tied up to poles. They shoot arrows at our hearts.

What happens?

They torture us.

Why do they do this?

Because we can't work no more. So tired. They beat us.

What's happening now?

(No answer.)

You can see it clearly. What's happening?

(No answer.)

Now it is all over. Can you feel your body there?

Uh-huh.

What did they do with it?

Bury it.

Does that bother you?

I can't feel it.

Are you glad that you got away from that?

Yup.

Do you feel better now?

Yup.

Now what do you do?

Just walkin'.

Where are you walking? Down on the ground near the bodies? How many people did they kill there?

Mmmm . . . they killed a lot of people.

Do you know what kind of people did all this?

I am not sure. We never hear things. All we do is get beat. They beat everybody.

All right, I am going to count to three. . . .

As a point of interest, after he had heard the tapes Carl testified that he had had a recurrent dream since early childhood in which he saw himself lying stretched out on a large rock slab with several arrows sticking from his body. He also told us that whenever he was under great physical or mental pressure or whenever he was especially fatigued, he would have nightmares in which he saw himself being forced to move large stones from what seemed to be an endless supply of rocks. Did Carl's regression give freedom and expression to long-buried subconscious memories of his death as a cavalry trooper and his life as a slave, or did his regression merely dramatize lives to fit the two recurrent dreams?

"I believe the day is not far away when people will have their family hypnotist as well as their family doctor and dentist," Bill said one evening after dinner.

"Sounds like an intriguing idea," I responded. "I imagine you're prepared to elaborate."

Bill motioned to Bryan, my oldest son, who put aside his magazine to come quickly to stand at Bill's side. The hypno-

tist's undisguised love of children and his friendly manner had
allowed him to establish control—sans hypnosis—over our
children within moments of his arrival.

"Bryan," he said, stroking his arm, "your arm is getting
numb. One, getting number; two, getting number still; three,
completely dead." He gave Bryan's arm a hearty pinch. "Did
you feel that?"

Bryan shook his head, smiled. "No, not a thing! How did
you do that?"

Bill laughed. "Now when I slap your arm with my finger,
all the feeling will come back." He lifted a forefinger, gave
Bryan's arm a light smack. "There. Back to normal, right?"

"Hey, neat!" Bryan pronounced, as if a minor miracle had
been accomplished.

"Well, you can do it too," Bill told him. "Try it. Stroke
your arm and count to three. Count to yourself. You don't
need to count out loud. Just tell yourself with every stroke
that your arm is getting more numb."

Bryan repeated the ritual, pinched his arm. "Hey!" he
declared. "It really works."

Nine-year-old Steve, my number two son, left his dessert
at the table and came into the living room to learn the
technique. He, too, found his arm completely numb at the
stroke of three. With Kari, however, it was a different story.
"No, thank you," she told Bill with a seven-year-old's serious-
ness. "I'm going to need my arm tonight. It mustn't be
numb."

"Well," Bill said, "that illustrates my point about the family hypnotist. Bryan and Steve were old enough to pick up the
trick themselves. Kari is just a bit young to really understand
what we were doing and to succumb to the power of suggestion.

"But let me illustrate further by taking a hypothetical
family in the year 1990. John and Mary Smith have two
children, Joe and Jane, both of whom were delivered pain-
lessly through natural chidlbirth abetted by hypnosis. John is
a successful salesman who owes much of his success to the
aggressiveness and self-confidence that he has developed

through periodic sessions with his hypnotist. Joe and Jane both maintain high marks in school, partly because their hypnotist has instilled in them a strong desire to learn. Both children enjoy their regular trips to the dentist because their hypnotist has removed their childish fear of his tools and he has trained them to anesthetize any part of their body at will.

"Last year when Joe broke his arm while playing football, he was able to remove the pain at once and to maintain this anesthetic effect while the arm was being set. This not only saved the family the expense of an anesthetist at the hospital, but spared Joe the unpleasant aftereffects of a regular anesthetic. Mary was able to go through a serious gall bladder operation without regular anesthetic, with the help of her hypnotist. Her recovery was especially rapid, because blood loss and shock were held to a minimum.

"Every three months each family member has a regularly scheduled visit with the hypnotist. During these visits post-hypnotic suggestions are given to renew and maintain their ability to eliminate pain in any part of their bodies at will. Through individual consultation, the hypnotist learns whether any member of the family has developed any bad habits, such as nail biting. If so, suggestions are given to remove the habit. Any other suggestions deemed necessary for the family's well-being are also given at this time. The children plan these visits to coincide with midyear and final exams at school. They have found that their recall is sharpened and their tensions reduced when the proper suggestions are given by the hypnotist.

"Their family doctor is very pleased that the Smiths visit their hypnotist regularly, because it makes his job easier. Troublesome allergies and other disorders of psychosomatic origin can be erased with a few hypnotic sessions, thus freeing the doctor to concentrate on organic disorders. The doctor has also found that medication, when needed, is much more effective with a patient who has been placed in a receptive state and has had his anxiety removed by a hypnotist."

"Your 'family hypnotist' hypothesis is not really that far-fetched, even by today's conservative standards," I remarked. "There are a good many clinical hypnotists around the country, and a good many medical men—especially dentists—who employ hypnosis. Who knows? We may not have to wait until 1990!"

The next afternoon Rita arrived for another session. Although she had proven to be an excellent "traveler," she had been unable to be regressed beyond the birth experience. That day, however, Rita plunged back into time to what appeared to have been an eleventh century life in the wooded mountainous area of Moravia. Because Rita's ancestry is Bohemian, her previous life may be deemed an example of genetic memory. On the other hand, because the entity seemed to have had no living children, Rita may have somehow dramatized a memory of a woman whom one of her ancestors might have known.

The other alternatives are, of course, that Rita's previous life is an interesting psychological phenomenon or that it is an actual memory of a former existence. As an observer to the regression, I can only testify that the emotions which Rita expressed while under hypnosis were very real. Whether they were stimulated by some interesting mental machinery or by some remembered remorse presents a question for perhaps endless debate. Here are excerpts from Rita's regression as "Jeeta" (a phonetic spelling):

You see some mountains. What are you doing?

Running.

Who are you?

A little girl.

What is your name?

I—I don't know.

Well, it isn't too important. Where do you live?

I don't know. There are a lot of mountains.

How old are you?

Around seven.

With whom do you live?

My father.

What does your father do?

He does many things. He's a carpenter, and he does many jobs for people. We have goats up in the hill. I watch the goats.

I'm going to count to three and you will be ten years old. Now what are you doing?

Working in the village.

What do you do in the village?

I sell things.

What is your name? I'll count to three and it will be very, very clear to you.

Jeeta.

Did you ever go to school, Jeeta?

No.

Did you ever learn to write anything?

No.

You can write your name, can't you?

I don't know.

Did you ever try it?

No.

Well, let's try it and see how it works. See if you can write your name for us. Here, write your name on this paper. (She makes childish scratches on the paper.)

How is your father these days?

Not so well.

What is the matter?

Sheep . . . the sheep and the goats died. He's not too well. I go visit him. I stay in the village.

What happened to the sheep and goats?

They got a disease. Sold most of them.

Do you get good food?

Yes. A lady makes bread and I take that to Father.

What kind of bread is this? What does it look like?

Just small.

What shape is the loaf?

Just to put in your hand.

What color is it?

Brown.

When I count to three it will be five years later. Now what are you doing, Jeeta?

I'm married now.

How old are you now?

Fifteen.

How long have you been married?

Two summers.

What is your husband's name?

(No answer)

You don't remember? What language do you speak? Let's hear you speak in your native language. Tell us that you are very happy to be here visiting with us.

(She speaks in what sounds like a Slavic tongue.)

Do you have any children?

A little boy.

What is his name?

Zerva.

How do you and your husband get along?

He is gone all day.

What does he do?

He goes to the next village.

What does he do for work?

He makes things and I help him make things and he goes to the next village to sell them.

What sort of things do you make?

Jewelry, bracelets and things like that.

Does it sell very well?

Not too well.

How much money can you make in a week?

Oh . . . six, seven coins.

I am going to count to three, and you are five years older. What are you doing?

Just walking in the hills.

Where are your children?

Boy works now. He helps make . . . make . . . wear. (Points to feet)

Shoes? What is the native word for this? (She answers in the other language.)

What is your husband doing now?
I don't know. I don't see him anymore.
When did he leave?
Never came back one day.
Did you ever try to find out what happened?
They said down at the next village he was gone.
Do you miss him?
Hmmmm. (Nods)
Where do you live now?
My boy helps me and I still make the bracelets.
Who sells them for you now?
I do.
Are you just as happy with your husband gone?
No.
What year is this?
(Long pause) *I'm not sure.*
It will come very clear to you. What year is it?
Tw—tw—tw. . . .
What is the name of the country in which you live?
Moravlu.
Do you know what year it is? (No answer) I'll count to three and it will be very clear to you.
Twel . . . twel . . . twelve.
Twelve what?
I don't know.
How old are you now?
Twenty-two.
I'm going to count to three and you will be thirty years old. What are you doing?
Traveling.
Where?
I don't know.
In what?
I have a cart.
Who is with you?
Where are you going? Why are you traveling?
Nobody.
Just to get away from home.

Are you going to stay away?

Nothing for me in the village.

Does it make you sad to leave the village?

(Nods)

Leave your boy behind, did you? He didn't want to go with you, or what?

(She begins to cry.) *He is dead!*

We are going to go on until you get settled in your new place. Now where are you? What are you doing?

Taking care of this family. Helping this lady.

How did you happen to get this job?

The lady felt sorry for me.

I see. She is a fine lady then. How many children do you have to take care of?

Three.

How long have you been here?

Not too long.

But you like it here. Better than the old village?

Yes. They're kind to me.

That's good. How old are you now?

Thirty-three.

All right. I am going to count to three and it will be ten years later. Now what are you doing?

Taking money.

For what? Selling something?

No.

What are you doing?

Taking it. —

Why?

I need money.

Do you want to get away?

Yes.

What happened to the family? The job you had?

The boy got hurt and I got the blame, so I want to go.

Was it your fault?

I should have been watching him and I wasn't.

So now you feel you should leave. Where are you going to go?

I don't know where I am going.

On the count of three it will be ten years later. Now what are you doing?

(Pause) *I don't know. I'm floating.*

Floating? What do you see?

Nothing.

Are you comfortable?

Yes.

Do you like this?

Yes.

Where is your body? Can you see it any place?

Just down there.

Where?

Down there.

So you're very comfortable now; you like this?

Uh-huh.

Now I am going to count to three. You will come back to the present. . . .

CHAPTER VIII

IF IT ISN'T REINCARNATION, WHAT COULD IT BE?

Psychic Psychodrama. A rather successful technique in the therapy of some kinds of mental illness is psychodrama, those spontaneous impersonations of the patient's problem in which he is given an opportunity to enact the conflicts which have inflamed his psyche. I have wondered if some of the cases suggestive of reincarnation might not be a kind of psychic psychodrama in which some segment of the subconscious seizes control of the subject during his regression and impersonates a fictitious personality for the purpose of providing insight into the darker recesses of the subject's character.

In cases in which an individual has made an accurate prediction of his contacting a particular disease, I have often felt that perhaps some transcendent level of his mind might have been subconsciously aware of the inroads of the disease upon the body quite some time before the overt symptoms of the illness began to manifest themselves. Perhaps during the individual's sleeping hours, when the conscious relaxes its control, the image of the disease may have been reproduced in the subject's dreams, thereby allowing him to "predict" the approach of the disease.

Could we have something of this sort in certain cases in which our regressed subjects recount what appear to have been other lives? Hypnosis frees the subconscious by simulating a sleep-like state which virtually anesthetizes the conscious mind. Perhaps regression permits a transcendent level of mind to dramatize some conflict of character, some weakness of moral fiber, or some approaching crisis by personifying itself as a previous physical embodiment of the present entity.

The fact that the regression personality is so often of a sex different from that of the entranced subject brings to mind Dr. C. G. Jung's theory of the *anima*, the female element in the male unconscious, and the *animus*, the male element in the female unconscious. In *Man and His Symbols*, M.-L. von Franz, a pupil of Jung, writes: " ... whenever one of these personifications of the unconscious takes possession of our mind, it seems as if we ourselves are having such thoughts and feelings. The ego identifies with them to the point where it is unable to detach them and see them for what they are. One is really 'possessed' by a figure from the unconscious."

Possession by Discarnate Entities. If it is not some element of the subject's own unconscious playing the role of a previous incarnation, then perhaps in certain cases suggestive of reincarnation a discarnate entity has invaded the psyche of the living, eager to tell its story to the hypnotist. Dr. Carl A. Wickland's *Thirty Years Among the Dead* recounts many such possessions and has, since its publication in 1924, become one of the classics in the literature of the paranormal.

There is the case of the Kentucky frontiersman, Dave Dean, who spoke through the mouth of William H. Thatcher, a trance medium, in Grand Rapids, Michigan. The spirit entity told of being born in the 1760's and having been a member of George Rogers Clark's expedition to Kaskaskia. It cited names, place names and facts which seem to indicate genuine memories of an actual physical existence in frontier America.

Mary Roff's possession of Lurancy Vennum has been chronicled in dozens of books on the paranormal. The Mary Roff entity borrowed Lurancy's body when she lay terribly ill of a fever and retained occupancy for a period of several months. Mary had died when Lurancy was only fifteen months old. Although both the Roffs and the Vennums lived in the same town of Watseka, Illinois, they were only slightly acquainted. Yet thirteen-year-old Lurancy, during the period of possession, displayed a knowledge of Mary's life and her personal habits which would have been far beyond the capacity of either Lurancy or her parents to mime.

There are many such documented cases of apparent spirit possession, including many which have occurred in contemporary times. Whenever I would propose possession as an alternative to reincarnation, Bill Williams would only shrug, admit the possibility, then add that he would have to discount it as a factor in any cases in which he had personally investigated. "I have yet to see any evidence of spirit possession," he would tell me.

All that changed on September 20, 1968, when a young sergeant, who had just been invalided home from Vietnam with several wounds, came to Bill with a story that he was being possessed by the spirit of a younger brother. Just a few months before, the sergeant, Ed, had been called home to attend the funeral of his fourteen-year-old brother, Marty, who was killed in a gun accident. Marty, who had stood six feet tall at the age of thirteen, was noted for his phenomenal physical strength. At the funeral, Ed said that he had felt the presence of Marty and had seemed to hear a whispered promise that Marty would "look after him."

After Marty's funeral, Ed returned to Vietnam where he was immediately involved in a serious battle. He was wounded, and blacked out. The young soldier may have been separated from his buddies and left for dead, but at this point Marty entered the body of the unconscious Ed and took control. With a speed and a strength which Ed had never possessed, and despite having been wounded in three places, he got himself to a hospital. Doctors were amazed when the severely wounded sergeant walked into the base. Ed remembers nothing after he blacked out from sustaining the wounds.

Now, the sergeant told Williams, it was apparent that Marty had saved his life, but it was also alarmingly apparent that Marty had liked the feel of a physical body once again. Ed had been conscious of Marty's constant presence and his repeated efforts to get into his body. Even as he sat talking to the hypnotist, the sergeant said, he could feel Marty's approach, which always was evidenced by a feeling of chill, prickly sensations and goose pimples on his skin.

Bill and his wife Elsie brought Ed with them to the home of Professor Charles Hapgood, a man of varied experience, who had dealt with cases of a similar nature in the past. In the Hapgood home, Bill placed Ed into trance. As soon as the young man was in deep trance, Marty took advantage of the situation to speak through his brother's vocal equipment.

The entity insisted that he only wished to protect Ed. Hapgood asked him if he did not realize how much his possessing Ed's body upset his brother. Marty said that he was unaware of making Ed feel uncomfortable and that he would continue to possess his body whenever he felt like it.

When Ed heard the tapes of Marty speaking through his mouth, he told Williams and Hapgood that he felt Marty wanted a test of strength. Marty had always been able to best his older brother in any contest of physical strength, but Ed felt that he now had the muscle power to win. He asked that Marty be allowed to take full possession for the contest. Williams and Hapgood counseled against such a test. Marty might not be so easy to pry out once he had taken full possession of a physical body. Ed continued to argue that Marty could only be bested in a physical contest.

"No sooner had Bill and I agreed to the experiment than Marty took over Ed's body right before our eyes," Professor Hapgood writes. "There was a complete change in the control of the body's action and in the facial expressions. The body now acted physically like the body of a fourteen-year-old boy. The features were contorted into the expressions of a rather petulant, frustrated child. The body stood up and tried to grasp and raise the heavy chair in front of it by one leg. It did a very poor job. It seated itself again and there was evidence of great agitation. . . . Marty said the test had been unfair, because Ed had been trying to push him out. He wanted another try. Reluctantly, Bill and I assented to this. First, however, we had Ed try to lift the chair, which he did without any trouble, holding it steadily above his head with one hand. (He was then not in trance, and he explained that Marty had previously been able to beat him in such a contest of strength.)

"We assented to the second test ... Marty took over Ed's body with grimacings and contortions that reminded Bill of nothing less than Dr. Jekyll and Mr. Hyde. He then arose from his chair and bent to pick up the other chair, but could scarcely get it off the ground. After violent efforts, he tried his other hand, but he couldn't do it."

Marty admitted to Bill that he had been bested in a fair test.

"What are you going to do now?" Bill asked the entity.

"I'm leaving," Marty said quietly. "I won't try to enter Ed's body again. But I'll come back again if ever he should need me."

Certain readers who have had a smattering of psychology in their academic careers will at once begin to theorize and conclude that the Marty-Ed case was just a rather dramatic case study in psychopathological phenomena. If one should study the literature of alleged "demon" and "spirit" possession, however, I think he would come to consider that there is something, perhaps as yet undefinable, but *something* more to such cases than neuroses running rampant.

Genetic Memory. In recent experiments with lower life forms, certain scientists have concluded that memory may be an inherited factor that is passed along in the genes together with determinants of height, weight and coloring. In an article in *Fate* magazine, Volney G. Mathison presented a genetic theory of reincarnation. Mathison speculates that certain repetitive dreams or hypnotically induced recollections of previous lives may really be the reactivated expressions of traumatic events suffered by an ancestor who passed the memory along in the genes.

In his article, Mathison cited a case in which a Mexican girl was in danger of losing her job due to her fear of fire.

Through preliminary analysis, Mathison determined that the girl had an intense subconscious fear of being burned. Conventional psychoanalytic theory would bid the therapist to search for the traumatic experience in childhood or infancy, but it was soon learned that the girl had never suffered severe burns in her life. While regressed, however, the girl told of being a Spanish immigrant coming to California on a crowded seventeenth century sailing vessel. Fire broke out, and the girl had been badly burned by a piece of flaming yardarm. Once the source of the girl's phobia had been discovered she could respond to therapy effectively.

Mathison discusses several other such cases from his personal research which illustrates his contention that since our electronic patterns transmit vital information about our ancestors' physical appearance, these same genetic patterns may also carry memory data which relate to enforced genetic modifications of structure which have occurred as a result of lack of food, injuries, plague and other disasters.

The theory of genetic memory as the principal contributing factor to cases suggestive of reincarnation seems to hold up quite well when the subject recalls an existence which took place in the land of his forebears. When a blond Scandinavian claims to remember a life as a Mongolian shepherd, however, the theory begins to crumble.

In *The Making of Man* Sir Oliver Lodge writes of heredity and reincarnation: "The heredity link appears to be of quite different order from the subliminal link; and mother and son need have no spiritual or subliminal relationship, in spite of their great similarity. The similarity of the body instrument would be sufficient, in that case, to account for the similarity of that portion of the son's larger self which automatically solicited this means of manifestation. And the importance of parenthood, in providing a suitable corporeal personality, can hardly be overestimated. But the indwelling spirit need not have come from the parents at all."

Delusions of Memory. We are all well aware that our recollections of certain facts and experiences may become either dimmed or distorted through the passage of time. Such errors and illusions of memory are quite familiar to all of us and nearly all of us have lost bets and arguments when our memory of a particular happening has been demonstrated to be incorrect. We shrug off such minor embarrassments. After all, no one has a perfect memory.

When however, some people recall what would seem to be a memory of a previous existence, they compound their error by adding interpretation to their faulty reproduction of a pseudo-memory. Let us illustrate by a hypothetical situation. We'll say that we are sitting around the fireplace some wintry evening discussing the fierce blizzard of '43. Suddenly our young friend, a schoolteacher in his mid-twenties, speaks up.

Yes, he says, he recalls the blizzard well. He remembers how the drifts were piled across the highways and how stranded motorists met grim deaths in the snow. His recollection of nights without electricity because of downed power-lines is vivid. He even sings a few lines from the songs that were popular that winter. We are puzzled for a few moments, then express our amazement that our friend is so old. Of course, he was quite young, he assures us, but he remembers it all very well. We ask precisely when he was born. August 25, 1944. A strange look crosses his face, and we need say no more. How could he remember so clearly an incident which took place before he was born?

There is no mystery here. As a young boy, very often he must have heard his relatives discuss the big blizzard of '43. Perhaps every Christmas when his parents took him with them to visit his grandparents there were whole evenings of reminiscences about the depth of the snow, how Uncle Mert, the salesman, got stranded and barely made it to the farm-house, how the children made tunnels in the huge drifts. Our young friend may have been sitting on the floor playing with his new Christmas toys, but yet he was hearing it all; and the grim but exciting tales were making indelible impressions on his subconscious. It would be natural for the young man to make the transition from listener to participant and subconsciously claim the memories for his own.

James H. Hyslop dealt with such delusions of memory in 1906 in his *Borderlands of Psychical Research*. Hyslop observed that our conscious memories seldom extend back beyond the age of four. "When they do they usually represent some isolated or striking event that impressed itself on our minds. Usually, however, the life of that early period is forgotten. . . . Now if at any time some event should occur which recalled enough of the experience previous to that which represents our present consciousness of personality to make us feel that it belonged to a time previous, and yet we could not recall any sense of personality corresponding to it, we might be excused for describing the facts as representing a previous existence. It would be a perfectly natural illusion."

Extrasensory Perception. In *The Power of Karma*, Alexander Cannon tells of a lady who was visiting Minnesota for the first time when the train on which she was traveling broke down. The woman remarked to her daughter that the farmland in which the mishap had occurred seemed familiar. When they got out to stretch their legs, the woman saw a farmhouse and told her daughter she was certain that she had lived there in another life. She described the arrangement of the house to the daughter; and since they had plenty of time, they walked up to the farmhouse and asked the owner if they might come in. There they found the interior of the home to be exactly as the mother had described it. The traveler related this incident to prove to her friends that reincarnation was a reality.

Cannon adds: "One of her friends was sufficiently interested to make inquiries about the farmhouse, and found that at the time of the woman's birth there had been no houses in the neighborhood. In this case it would appear that the lady in question was able to describe the house by means of the sense perception we call psychometry, an extension of normal consciousness."

Rev. Leslie D. Weatherhead's *The Case for Reincarnation* quotes a letter from a correspondent who tells how her son

David became excited at the excavation site of a Roman villa and began to speak as if he had lived there. The boy finally asked to be taken away because he could not bear the rush of memories which saddened him. When they visited some caves in Guernsey which had once served as prisons for French soldiers, the boy tapped on the walls until he found a spot which he insisted covered a smaller cave where a prisoner had been walled in. The boy even gave the prisoner's name and number.

Reverend Weatherhead's correspondent wrote: "Eventually, steps were taken and the walls were tapped for any thin place which could have been the outline of a door. The door was found: it had been bricked up. Stretched out on the floor was the skeleton of a man. When the archives were searched, the name David had given was correct."

David had also experienced an unusual reaction when his mother took him to the British Museum to view some recently acquired mummies. The boy calmly peered inside a sarcophagus and told his mother that there should have been three initials on the underside of the case. He made three birds on a note pad and told his mother that had been his name in that life in Egypt, during which time he had served as an inspector of sarcophagi.

Reverend Weatherhead is of the opinion that such strange "memories" have "no adequate interpretation other than that of reincarnation."

In my book *The Enigma of Reincarnation*, after discussing David's case at some length I concluded: "It would seem to me to be stretching the laws of chance a bit too far to consider that a young boy from London could happen to arrive in Naples just as his former villa was being excavated, tour the caves in Guernsey where he had served either as guard or prisoner, and happen to come into contact with the one sarcophagus among thousands [that would contain his initials as inspector]. It seems much more realistic to suppose that David and his parents were unaware of the fact that he possessed a great talent for psychometry."

Now that we have examined some alternate theories to the reincarnation hypothesis, some skeptics are going to feel a bit better about the whole business because they have, perhaps, singled out one particular theory which seems logical to them and which will allow them to put the greater question once again out of their minds. I know the feeling. I have experienced it myself.

My favorite theory used to be genetic memory, but that went up like dry tinder against too many contrary sparks. In order to be able to utilize genetic memory as a satisfactory explanation for cases suggestive of reincarnation, it is necessary to establish a geneological relationship between the subject and the entity who claims to have lived the former life reactivated during the regression experience. In the overwhelming majority of cases, this simply cannot be done.

Delusions of memory may certainly explain many of the common "I've been here before" sensations which nearly everyone experiences from time to time. Delusions of memory may even explain certain instances in which a subject claims to remember a life immediately preceeding his present existence. In my opinion, however, the theory crumbles pretty rapidly against even the most superficial evidence unearthed in most of the cases suggestive of reincarnation with which I am familiar.

I am convinced that possession—mental, spirit, "demon"—does occur, but in no case of possession with which I am familiar does the entity claim to represent a former life of the subject whose physical frame it has inhabited. The possessing entity is an invader (and usually makes no bones about it), not a reactivated memory pattern.

Because of my many years investigating "psi" (ESP) abilities of the human mind, it is very hard for me to let go of clairvoyance, telepathy and psychometry as being the principal contributors to many cases suggestive of reincarnation. And becuase I think the creative potential of the human psyche is virtually unlimited, I find that a good number of cases could also be left at the doorstep of psychic psychodrama.

But there are always those stubborn cases that resist any theory other than the heretical, unspeakable doctrine of reincarnation. If clairvoyance provided George Field, the New Hampshire schoolboy, with information about the life of Jonathan Powell, a man who had died more than one hundred years before in a faraway southern village, then young George's "psi" abilities must be developed to a degree which would enable him to pick up messages from a distant locale concerning a man long dead. In order for a telepathic percipient to receive impressions, some living agent has to be "broadcasting." This means that a great many villagers in Jefferson, North Carolina, must have had Jonathan Powell on their minds at all times and were constantly "transmitting" psychic impressions of his life and colorful times. As we know, Jonathan Powell lived and died in obscurity. When Williams investigated in Jefferson, there was no one who had ever heard of the young farmer who had been shot in the market place by the "Yankees."

Once George Field had been brought to Jefferson, one might make some kind of case for the "psi" hypothesis, but it would be a very weak one. Why should George have singled out the farmer Jonathan for the object of his clairvoyance? Could Jonathan's murder have so supercharged the psychic ether in Jefferson that the impressions of this single act of atrocity reached out and touched a psychically sensitive teenager over one hundred years later? But if this were true, the impressions must have reached all the way to New Hampshire, and we have endowed George Field with superhuman powers of mind.

Clearly, in the case of Jonathan Powell and a good many of the other cases detailed in this book, there is more at work than ESP, genetic memory, spirit possession, psychic psychodrama and delusions of memory. Can we, as products of twentieth century Western culture, admit that reincarnation might well be that something more?

CHAPTER IX

OTHER RESEARCH AND INVESTIGATION INTO THE ENIGMA OF REINCARNATION

"Nobody has as yet thought up a way that reincarnation could be proved in a laboratory test tube. But even in the laboratory we cannot escape from human testimony of some kind or other. In studying cases of reincarnation, I have to use the methods of the historian, lawyer, psychiatrist. I gather testimony from as many people as possible," Dr. Ian Stevenson, Chairman of the Department of Neurology and Psychiatry at the School of Medicine of the University of Virginia, told reporter Doug Laurie.

Dr. Stevenson has done more to put the study of reincarnation on a scientific basis than any other single individual. Certainly his academic and professional credits should convince even the most hostile skeptic that he is a man who would not be inclined to make rash judgments and crude assessments. At this point in his investigation, Dr. Stevenson's principal contributions have been "The Evidence for Survival from Claimed Memories of Former Incarnations," the winning essay in the American Society of Psychical Research's 1960 contest in honor of William James, and his *Twenty Cases Suggestive of Reincarnation*, which was published by the ASPR in 1966.

In an analysis of the material with which he worked while compiling his winning essay, Dr. Stevenson discusses several hypotheses which he feels deserve consideration in attempting to comprehend data from cases suggestive of reincarnation. Among these hypotheses are the following:

Unconscious Fraud. Dr. Stevenson points out that in some cases other persons have attributed statements to the subject which he never made and in this way have permitted the initial story to grow out of proportion. The researcher terms this a kind of "collective hallucination" in which further statements are imaginatively attributed to the subject. Dr. Stevenson makes a very interesting point when he tells the reader that simply because so many of these cases suggestive of reincarnation have occurred in cultures where the populace accepts the doctrine of rebirth, one should not believe that the Hindus and Buddhists encourage their children to remember previous lives. On the contrary, he states, they consider it tragic if a child remembers a former existence, for this, they believe, presages an early death. Oriental parents often violently discourage their children from speaking of their alleged memories.

Derivation of the "Memories" Through Normal Means with Subsequent Forgetting of the Source. The researcher holds this hypothesis to be most often responsible for the many cases of psuedo-reincarnation. "We need to remember that we can acquire knowledge and subsequently forget our source of acquisition while recalling the facts learned," Dr. Stevenson points out.

He also quotes from the work of E. S. Zolik, who studied the ability of subjects to create fictitious former lives while under hypnosis. These fantasy personalities were the products of bits and pieces of characters in novels and movies and remembered childhood acquaintances. Because of the remarkable ability of the human mind to acquire paranormal information and to create fantasy personalities all its own, Dr. Stevenson cites yet another difficulty in serious research in cases suggestive of reincarnation: "We need to remember that items normally acquired can become mingled with those paranormally derived in the productions of persons apparently remembering past lives."

Racial Memory. Dr. Stevenson, a medical doctor as well

as a psychiatrist, is well aware that man has not yet discovered the limits of genetic transmission. He feels, however, that such a theory applied to the alleged memories of previous lives which have survived investigation will encounter serious obstacles. He concedes that the hypothesis might apply in instances where it can be shown that the percipient of the memories belongs to a line descending from the personality whom he claims to be. But in most cases, the separation of time and place makes " ... impossible any transmission of information from the first to the second person along genetic lines."

Extrasensory Perception of the Items of the Apparent Recollections in the Minds of Living Persons. Dr. Stevenson finds it difficult to accept the notion that an individual gifted with paranormal talents should limit the exercise of such abilities only to communication with the specific living persons who had relevant items of information concerning the deceased personality from whom the subject claims to derive his memories. (Dr. Stevenson has usually limited himself to cases in which the percipient is a small child who is able to be transported among those people who knew the deceased personality in life. In cases in which the previous personality has been dead for a hundred years and all his friends, relatives and associates have also passed away, the ESP hypothesis almost completely falls apart, except, as we have already noted, for such talents as psychometry making the clairvoyant seem a part of a scene of the past.)

Retrocognition. The researcher speaks of the question of this "psi" ability being responsible for cases suggestive of reincarnation by reminding us that the subject in such cases is always " ... (a) at the scene of the retrocognized events, e.g., in Salisbury Cathedral; or (b) stimulated by some object connected with the events themselves or persons participating in them. . . ; or (c) in an altered state of consciousness, e.g., gazing at a crystal or in a trance." Such conditions do not, of course, apply to the great majority of cases in which an individual claims memories of a former existence.

Possession. Dr. Stevenson concedes that cases such as that of Lurancy Vennum seem to "... make plausible the hypothesis of temporary possession as an explanation for apparent memories of former incarnations." But in cases of possession, he tells the reader, the entity that has accomplished the transformation of personality usually does so solely for the purpose of communication with its loved ones on the physical plane and it never claims to be a former incarnation of the subject who has temporarily housed it. In true cases suggestive of reincarnation, there is no other personality claiming to occupy the body of the subject and the entity speaks of a former life, not of communication with surviving loved ones.

Dr. Stevenson believes that his accumulated evidence justifies "... a much more extensive and more sympathetic study of [reincarnation] than it has hitherto received in the West. Further investigation of apparent memories of former incarnations may well establish reincarnation as the most probable explanation of these experiences." Dr. Stevenson points out that in attempting to prove survival by evaluating mediumistic communications "... we have the problem of proving that someone clearly dead still lives." In shifting the emphasis of research toward an investigation of apparent memories of previous incarnations "... the problem consists in judging whether someone clearly living once died. This may prove to be the easier task and, if pursued with sufficient zeal and success, may contribute decisively to the question of survival."

We must not overlook the work of the Association for Research and Enlightenment, which, under the directorship of Hugh Lynn Cayce, has carried on the work of the celebrated Edgar Cayce. The work of Edgar Cayce is too well known to require elaboration in this book, but any researcher who has approached this work with an orthodox, but open, mind receives a powerful shock of recognition when he reads how the deeply religious seer of Virginia Beach felt upon hearing that he had spoken seriously and in depth of the doctrine of rebirth.

In *Edgar Cayce on Reincarnation*, author Noel Langley writes that when Cayce, "the most devout and orthodox of Protestants, a man who had read the Bible once for each of his forty-six years" heard his secretary read a transcript of the session he had just completed with a gentleman named Arthur Lammers, he was both frightened and bewildered. In trance, Cayce had stated ". . . flatly and emphatically that, far from being a half-baked myth, the law of reincarnation was a cold, hard fact."

Cayce's first fear, Langley tells us, was that ". . . his subconscious faculties had suddenly been commandeered by the forces of evil, making him their unwitting tool; and he had always vowed that if ever his clairvoyant powers were to play him false, he would permit no further use of them."

From 1925 through 1944 Edgar Cayce gave 2,500 readings which dealt with the Karmic patterns that had arisen out of the previous existences of those individuals who had sought out the seer's psychic assistance. To read even a part of the records of those readings is to be continually amazed at the enormous amount of substantiative information and details which were discovered in a great many of the cases.

CHAPTER X

THE ETHICS OF KARMA: REINCARNATION AS A
PHILOSOPHY OF LIFE

"You enter a human body for a purpose. If you follow natural law, if you care for your body, if you take precautions necessary to safeguard the vehicle through which your soul is expressing, you stay within that body until that purpose is fulfilled. You, at that time, leave the body; and you come into spirit. You pass through the change man calls death—the transition from your world into the spirit world.

"Man has long looked at this transition as a mystery, as the greatest of all mysteries; but, I say to you, it is no mystery. When the time comes for you to leave your earthly body and once again take up the spiritual body, you step from the old into the new; and many times do not even know the transition has been made. . . . It is no mystery; it is no change. The great change is when a spiritual being in the spirit world must diminish his spiritual form and come back within the body of a newborn babe to once again live his purpose upon the earth, knowing not why he is there. . . . When you think of the many people that have been expressed in physical bodies, you will know that, when a spirit enters a body, it must be because of divine plan. It must be for a reason, and I would like to try to make clear to you what we spirits speak of, know, and understand to be reincarnation."

Counsel from the spirit world. . . . The above has been quoted from a lecture on reincarnation and Karma which was given by the spirit teacher White Lily through the trance mediumship of Reverend Margaret L. Fling, White Lily Chapel, Ashley, Ohio.

"How many reincarnations are made," White Lily says, "depends entirely upon the spirit manifesting and upon the free will it exercises; for some spirits do not stray very far from the great Creator, the God force, and they are able in very few reincarnations to return—perfected individuals. Others must return over and over again, for they are not apt pupils. . . .

"God's plan, natural law, is a constant progression, either within the material world or within the spiritual world. It is progression; it must be. There may be, and there have been, periods of recession; but, in comparison with eternity, they were as a wink of the eye in time. Man has progressed steadily upward. That is the plan; that is the law that is leading him. He cannot deviate from it, and however many earth lives are needed for him to attain it, that many shall he live through. . . ."

(On Karma) "If you . . . have absorbed the understanding that God is love; that as you sow, so shall you reap; that as you plant, so gather you in; you will know that there is no punishment. You are not punished for the deeds you have committed, either in this life, or in the life to come. They are shown to you, clear and defined, and then you are left free to work out the mistakes of the past. As I say, it is not punishment visited upon you; it is but the natural working of God's law; it is but cause and effect in operation. . . .

The cycle of rebirth is discussed, evaluated and accepted in the most ancient texts of all cultures. The *Hermes Trismegistus*, which set forth the esoteric doctrines of the ancient Egyptian priesthood, recognizes the reincarnation of "impious souls" and the achievement of pious souls when they know God and become "all intelligence." It decrees against transmigration, the belief that the soul of men may enter into animals. "Divine law preserves the human soul from such infamy," state the Hermetic books.

The *Bhagavad-Gita*, holy text of the Hindus, observes:

As the dweller in the body experienceth in the body childhood, youth, old age, so passeth he on to another body; the steadfast one grieveth not thereat. . . .

He who regardeth himself as a slayer, or he who thinketh he is slain, both of them are ignorant. He slayeth not, nor is he slain.

He is not born, nor does he die; nor having been, ceaseth he any more to be; unborn, perpetual, eternal and ancient, he is not slain when the body is slaughtered.

As a man, casting off worn-out garments, taketh new ones, so the dweller in the body, casting off worn-out bodies, entereth into others that are new. . . .

For certain is death for the born, and certain is birth for the dead; therefore over the inevitable thou shouldst not grieve.

Our Judaeo-Christian heritage is hardly devoid of the doctrine of reincarnation. The great leader Josephus admonished some Jewish soldiers, who wished to kill themselves rather than be captured by the Romans, with these words: "Do ye remember that all pure Spirits who are in conformity with the divine dispensation live on in the lowliest of heavenly places, and in course of time they are again sent down to inhabit sinless bodies; but the souls of those who have committed self-destruction are doomed to a region in the darkness of the underworld?"

In his *Lux Orientalis*, Joseph Glanvil states that man's pre-existence was a philosophy commonly held by the Jews; this is illustrated by the disciples' ready questioning of Jesus when they asked: "Master, was it for this man's sin or his father's that he was born blind?" If the disciples had not believed that the blind man had lived another life in which he might have sinned, Glanvil argues, the question would have been senseless and impertinent. When Christ asked his disciples who men said He was, they answered that some said John the Baptist, others Elias, others Jeremiah or one of the prophets. Glanvil reasons that such a response on the part of the disciples demonstrates their belief in metempsychosis and pre-existence. "These, one would think, were very proper occasions for our Savior to have rectified His mistaken followers had their supposition been an error. . . ."

Andre Pezzani takes issue with the Christian doctrine of man's original sin in *The Plurality of the Soul's Existence*: "Original sin does not account for the particular fate of individuals, as it is the same for all. . . ." Once man accepts the theory of pre-existence, Pezzani holds, ". . . a glorious light is thrown on the dogma of sin, for it becomes the result of personal faults from which the guilty soul must be purified. Pre-existence, once admitted as regards the past, logically implies a succession of future existences for all souls that have not yet attained to the goal, and that have imperfections and defilements from which to be cleansed. In order to enter the *circle of happiness* and leave the *circle of wanderings*, one must be pure."

In the opinion of Eva Gore-Booth, such is the role that Christ assumes in God's Great Plan—to offer man release from the cycle of rebirth. Christ came to offer eternal life to all men, ". . . a deliverance from reincarnation, from the life and death circle of this earthly living, not from any torments of a bodiless state, but simply from the body of this death." In *A Psychological and Poetic Approach to the Study of Christ in the Fourth Gospel*, she writes: "The idea of a succession of lives and deaths, following one another, for those who have not yet attained real life—are not yet Sons of God and children of the Resurrection—seems to illuminate, in a curious way, some of Christ's most profound and seemingly paradoxical teaching on the destiny and the hope, the life or death of the human psyche."

Origen (185 A.D. to 254 A.D.) devoted his life to the preservation of the original gospels. A prolific Christian writer, Origen maintained a relationship between faith and knowledge and explained the sinfulness of all men by the doctrine of the pre-existence of all souls.

"Is it not rational that souls should be introduced into bodies in accordance with their merits and previous deeds, and that those who have used their bodies in doing the utmost possible good should have a right to bodies endowed with qualities superior to the bodies of others?" he asked in *Contra Celsum*. "The soul, which is immaterial and invisible in its nature, exists in no material place without having a body suited to the nature of that place; accordingly, it at one time puts off one body, which is necessary before, but which is no longer adequate in its changed state, and it exchanges it for a second."

In the *De Principiis*, Origen stated that ". . . every soul . . . comes into this world strengthened by the victories or weakened by the defeats of its previous life. Its place in this world as a vessel appointed to honor or dishonor is determined by its previous merits or demerits. Its work in this world determines its place in the world which is to follow this. . . . I am indeed of the opinion that as the end and consummation of the saints will be in those [ages] which are not seen and are eternal, we must conclude that rational creatures had also a similar beginning. . . . And if this is so, then there has been a descent from a higher to a lower condition, on the part not only of those souls who have deserved the change . . . but also on that of those who, in order to serve the whole world, were brought down from those higher and invisible spheres to these lower and visible ones. . . . The hope of freedom is entertained by the whole of creation—of being liberated from the corruption of slavery—when the sons of God, who either fell away or were scattered abroad, shall be gathered into one, and when they shall have fulfilled their duties in this world."

At the Council of Nicaea in 325 A.D., Origenism was excluded from the doctrines of the Church and fifteen anathemas were proposed against Origen. The Origenists had lost by only one vote, but, as stated by Head and Cranston in *Reincarnation, An East-West Anthology*, ". . . Catholic scholars are beginning to disclaim that the Roman Church took any part in the anathemas against Origen. . . . However, one disastrous result of the mistakes still persists; namely, the exclusion from the Christian creed of the teaching of the pre-existence of the soul, and, by implication, reincarnation."

(For an excellent summation of how the doctrine of reincarnation was removed from the *Bible*, see *Edgar Cayce on Reincarnation* by Noel Langley.

It seems now that once again man is willing to consider that it is his transcendental self, his basic essence, which has introduced him into life and has determined his particular individuality. Whatever earthly misery he may confront, the man who has come to recognize the transcendental spark within himself will see that such suffering is for his own transcendental advantage. Those who have glimpsed a bit of the transcendental self have come to know that man is his own heir, that what man has gained morally and intellectually remains with him.

"A man has a soul, and it passes from life to life, as a traveler from inn to inn, till at length it is ended in heaven," H. Fielding Hall wrote in *The Soul of a People*. "But not till he has attained heaven in his heart will he attain heaven in reality."

Perhaps no one has expressed the ethics of Karma and presented reincarnation as a philosophy of life better than did Gina Cerminara in *Many Mansions*. In Chapter XXIV, "A Philosophy to Live By," Dr. Cerminara, a trained psychologist, presents the essence of the wisdom which she received from an extensive study of the Edgar Cayce readings while residing at Virginia Beach.

In outline form this pattern seems to be as follows:

God exists.
Every soul is a portion of God.
   (You *are* a soul; you inhabit a body.)
Life is purposeful.
Life is continuous.
All human life operates under law.
   (Karma; reincarnation)
Love fulfills that law.
The will of man creates his destiny.
The mind of man has formative power.
The answer to all problems is within the Self.

In accordance with the above postulates, man is enjoined as follows:

> Realize first your relationship to the Creative Forces of the Universe, or God.
> Formulate your ideals and purposes in life.
> Strive to achieve those ideals.
> Be active.
> Be patient.
> Be joyous.
> Leave the results to God.
> Do not seek to evade any problem.
> Be a channel of good to other people.

E. D. Walker portrayed the doctrine of reincarnation very well when he said that it unites all the family of man into a universal brotherhood. Reincarnation ". . . promotes the solidarity of mankind by destroying the barriers that conceit and circumstances have raised between individuals, groups, nations, and races. There are no special gifts . . . successes are the laborious result of long merit . . . failures proceed from negligence. The upward road to . . . spiritual perfection is always at our feet. . . . The downward way to sensual wreckage is but the other direction of the same way. We cannot despise those who are tending down, for who knows but we have journeyed that way ourselves? It is impossible for us to scramble up alone, for our destiny is included in that of humanity, and only by helping others along can we ascend ourselves."

Perhaps a fitting close to a study of the claimed memories of former lives might be found in the personal creed of Friedrich Nietzsche: "Live so that thou mayest desire to live again—that is thy duty; for in any case, thou wilt live again!"

THE END

Mankind's oldest mystery—immortality through reincarnation—is explored in an unusual and disturbing book . . .

REINCARNATION

Hans Stefan Santesson

To what extent does a previous life, or lives, affect a person now? What part of a human being can be reincarnated—and what cannot? These and many other questions are answered in a series of fascinating case studies.

A482

WITCHCRAFT IN THE WORLD TODAY
U. H. Wallace

Explore the fascinating world of witchcraft . . . learn about love potions . . . share in orgiastic voodoo ceremonies . . . discover the incredible extent of belief in "The Evil Eye."

A269

WEBSTER'S NEW HANDY POCKET DICTIONARY

An Award Books Special

With its illustrations throughout, its special section of new words that are "on probation" in our modern language, its automatic pronouncing key, and other features, this remains the #1 compact guide.

A364